Fundamental Principles
Intermediate
Literacy and Numeracy

Susan M Green

Illustrations by Nguyen Matthias and Christy Martin

ISBN: 9781864765496

Copyright © Axiom Publishing, 2008, Reprinted 2009
Unit 2, 1 Union Street, Stepney, South Australia, 5069.

Axiom
Australia
www.axiompublishing.com.au
Printed in Malaysia

Spelling

Before We Start:

In English, every alphabet letter has a name and a sound. The first letter in the alphabet a is called ay as in May but is sounded...a as in cat. Digraphs are 2 letters which when together make a new sound which is different from either of the original single sounds.

For example t (as in it) and h (as in hat) when put together make the new sound th (as in thick). Digraphs form important word families and when recognised can help with learning to read/ spell/say a word. Some th words are 'with'; 'thick'; 'thin' and 'mother'. In each case the t and h together make a special sound. As you go through this book, Professor Mentor will introduce you to more of these sounds.

ee   e + e = ee

word list: see   tree   three   knee   bee   week   green   feet   sweet
sheet   keep   sleep   sheep   weed   feed

Write all of the list words in dictionary order.

1 _____   2 _____   3 _____

4 _____   5 _____   6 _____

7 _____   8 _____   9 _____

10 _____   11 _____   12 _____

13 _____   14 _____   15 _____

I see a bee
on a weed
looking to
feed on
something sweet.

Write sentences using these words: three, feet. sleep

_____

_____

_____

Draw three sheep asleep on their
feet under a tree.

Write in the feet all the ee words you have
learned.

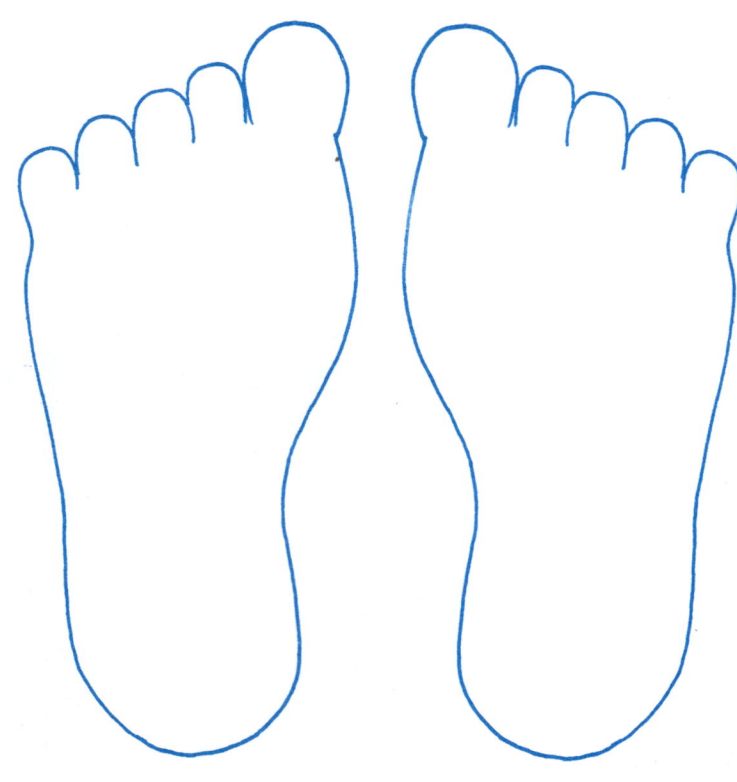

2

wh w + h = wh

These words ask a question: when, where, why, which
Write a question using each of these words
Professor Mentor asks — 'What comes at the end to show it is a question?'

_____

_____

_____

_____

Which words fit here?

_ _ i_ e   _ _ _ el   _ _ i _ _   _ _ i s _ _ r   _ _ _ c h   _ _ e _ .

Draw a picture for these words:

Whip	Wheel

Which word from the word list
fits into this shape?

Write in the whale all
the wh words you
have learned.

3

sh   s + h = sh

word list: shop   shut   ship   shed   shell   she   wish   fish   dish   brush
clash   dash   splash

From the word list choose the best word
to fit in each of these sentences:

While at the beach she found a beautiful
_____ on the sand.

He made a fast _____ out of the rain.

One day I would like to travel on a _____ .

Her mother told her to _____ her hair.

From the word list choose the words
that rhyme with:

dish   dash

_____   _____

_____   _____

Professor Mentor asks:
'Do you know other words which also rhyme
with these?'

_____   _____

_____   _____

_____   _____

Find the words from the word list.

S	H	U	T	J	O	K	J	P	B	X	X
Y	S	F	N	X	I	U	J	S	K	J	K
F	H	W	W	M	R	N	V	H	P	K	Z
Y	E	Q	W	T	Y	W	A	E	A	R	G
I	D	O	D	A	S	H	K	L	G	B	W
S	F	F	I	S	H	G	N	L	P	E	V
P	W	G	S	M	X	F	G	X	D	X	I
L	B	H	A	T	O	H	G	S	P	S	E
A	X	J	N	I	S	C	Y	H	K	S	J
S	B	X	I	I	M	L	Q	E	K	H	H
H	D	R	W	Q	N	A	C	D	L	O	P
D	S	J	U	W	V	S	I	H	W	P	W
Y	H	S	B	S	D	H	S	Y	R	L	V
G	I	K	S	O	H	I	Q	R	X	V	U
E	P	K	J	Y	D	H	G	P	P	G	Y

Write in the dish all the sh words you
have learned.

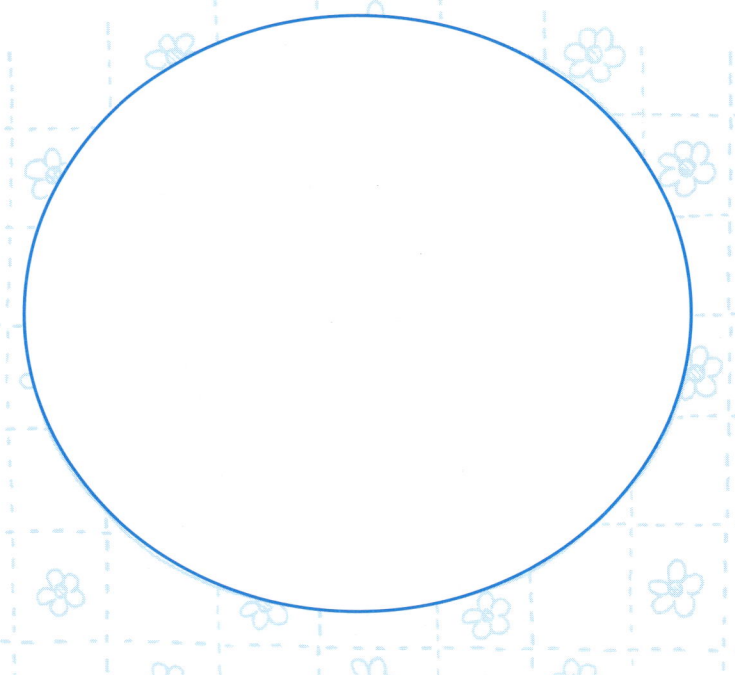

A fun **sh** tongue twister.

She sells sea shells by the sea shore.
The shells she sells are surely seashells.
So if she sells shells on the seashore,
I'm sure she sells seashore shells.

4

ch   c + h = ch

word list: chip   chop   chicken   cherry   cheese   children   rich   bunch
lunch   pinch   catch   match

Professor Mentor asks, 'Which words from the word list fit into these shapes?'

Which word from the word list means:

To cut firewood. _____

The second meal of the day. _____

To grasp a ball. _____

Things which look alike. _____

Use three list words in your own sentences:

_____

_____

_____

Fill in the missing list words: lunch, catch, children, cheese

The _____ had a _____ sandwich for _____, and then went out to play

_____.

A fun **ch** tongue twister.

Charlie chews cherry cheese while
chasing Chinese chickens
around the
charred chimney.

Tom's Lunchbox

Write in the lunch box all the ch words
that you have learned.

5

ar   a + r = ar

word list: star   car   party   park   farm   card   arm   bark   jar   far
arch   art   dark   start

Using these words add the ending   s, ed, ing.

star   _____

park   _____   _____   _____

bark   _____   _____   _____

start   _____   _____   _____

Professor Mentor suggests you pretend being a pirate. Dress up as a pirate. What do you say when you are a pirate? "Aaaaarrrr!"

Which list words are shown in these pictures?

_____   _____   _____

Find the words from the word list.

F	O	U	J	S	G	X	E	W	P	H	W
F	I	V	R	E	G	C	P	Y	A	L	L
J	C	A	N	M	I	A	A	T	R	T	M
F	T	A	Q	E	O	R	R	H	T	E	E
S	T	R	I	B	X	D	K	M	Y	T	N
D	D	M	R	P	Y	J	G	C	X	A	R
G	W	B	A	E	V	O	U	A	R	R	F
O	I	S	F	P	S	T	A	R	T	C	I
S	D	U	A	M	K	W	D	N	Y	H	C
L	Q	B	R	S	N	D	A	J	B	T	Y
T	J	X	N	E	Z	F	R	G	A	S	Q
J	A	R	S	E	Y	A	K	S	R	M	Y
D	A	Z	B	J	S	R	L	Y	K	S	B
I	W	R	W	P	S	M	H	X	I	R	R
J	L	Q	T	X	V	J	N	B	W	A	V

Write in the star all the ar words you have learned.

6

th   t + h = th

Circle the th part of these words.

th tongue twister

I thought a thought.
But the thought I thought
wasn't the thought
I thought I thought.

then	thick	thin
that	thing	thank
bath	this	both
think	moth	with

Which list words are shown in these pictures?

 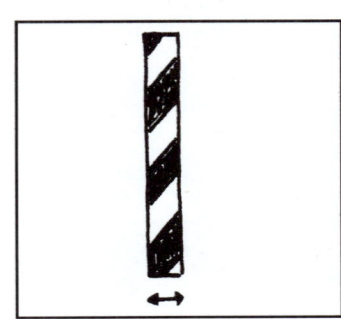 

Write a sentence using these words: this, that

_____

Join the number to the word.

8th	fifth
6th	tenth
10th	ninth
9th	eighth
5th	sixth

Write in the bath all the th words you have learned.

Find the words from the word list.

V	F	L	M	B	T	H	A	T	W	X	C
C	B	J	J	O	V	L	Z	T	W	N	Q
T	H	I	N	K	J	B	R	H	H	D	B
Z	R	A	E	Y	S	W	P	I	K	U	M
G	L	A	I	K	L	O	F	N	C	D	D
V	A	T	T	H	A	N	K	G	U	K	F
R	H	J	R	H	Y	A	H	O	O	T	Y
T	H	E	N	T	U	P	R	K	T	H	D
E	V	K	G	H	B	B	P	Z	H	I	U
W	B	O	N	I	A	M	W	Q	I	N	K
G	L	O	L	S	T	O	I	K	C	S	P
C	F	P	T	Y	H	T	T	B	K	D	S
Q	N	U	D	H	Q	H	H	K	V	V	D

q this always says q

q must always have its best friend u

Which word from the word list means:

The sound a duck makes. _____

Something on your bed to keep you warm. _____

She wears a crown on her head. _____

Which word from the word list means:

The opposite of noisy. _____

If you ask it you get an answer. _____

Hurry up. _____

Circle the correct word.

I can run quiet / quite quickly.

Sam ate a quarter / quiz of the cake.

Kate made a query / quiche for dinner.

A Quokka

A marsupial living in Western Australia.

Which list words fit the sentence?
quite, quiet, quarter

I asked her to be _____.

She was _____ naughty.

He ate a _____ of a pizza.

Find the words from the word list.

V	I	Q	J	I	P	N	H	U	I	W	Y
S	Q	R	V	Q	P	J	C	C	X	R	V
I	U	W	M	U	X	Z	H	K	E	B	D
I	I	Q	R	I	W	X	S	U	E	K	D
A	N	O	U	Z	S	I	Q	E	Q	Q	U
B	C	Q	A	E	Q	L	Z	K	U	P	K
L	H	H	V	B	S	U	Q	U	E	Q	N
A	E	Q	U	I	L	T	I	S	E	U	O
F	S	K	Q	M	R	X	I	E	N	A	A
S	S	T	L	W	X	Q	H	O	T	R	Z
R	V	E	B	Q	U	A	C	K	N	T	I
I	P	D	X	P	B	D	Y	U	N	E	X
W	V	Q	U	I	C	K	G	T	F	R	D

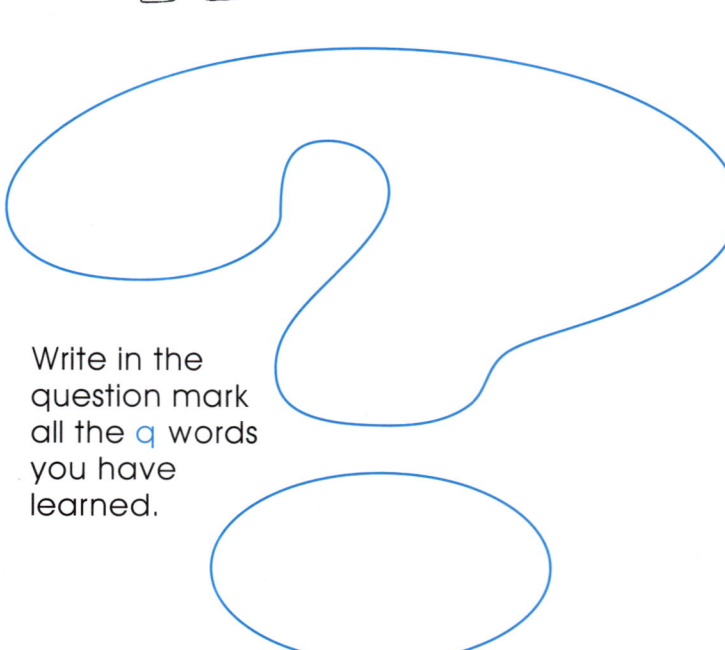

Write in the question mark all the q words you have learned.

8

er   e + r = er

word list: her utter dinner letter father mother sister brother under over fern bigger smaller

Professor Mentor asks, 'Which words from the word list fit into these shapes?'

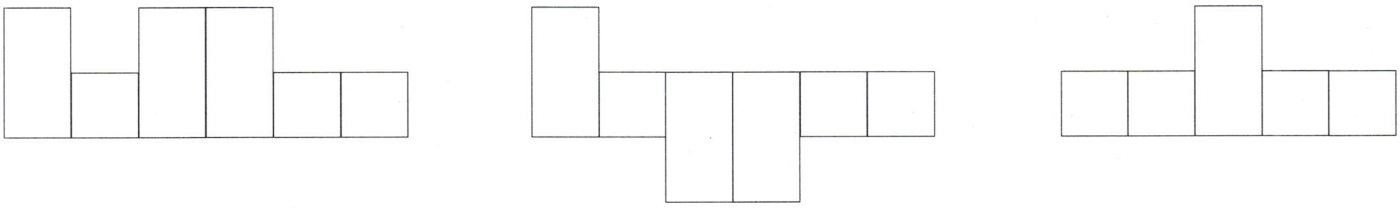

Father, mother, sister and brother are in families.
Draw your family members and name them.

Choose the word that best fits:

The cow jumped __________ the moon.

She slid __________ the fence.

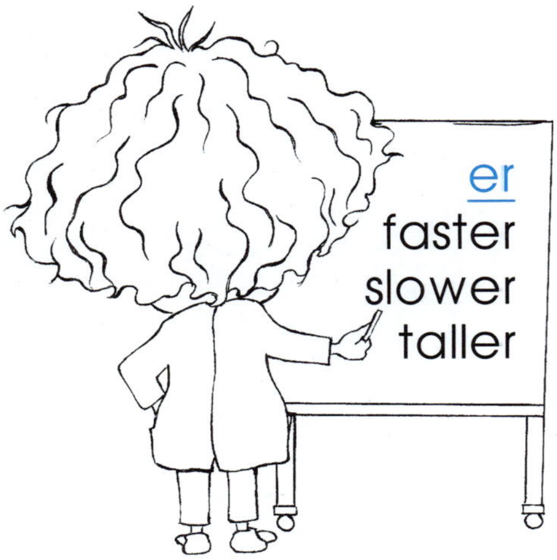

er
faster
slower
taller

Write on the letter all the er words you have learned.

Mrs. White
50¢

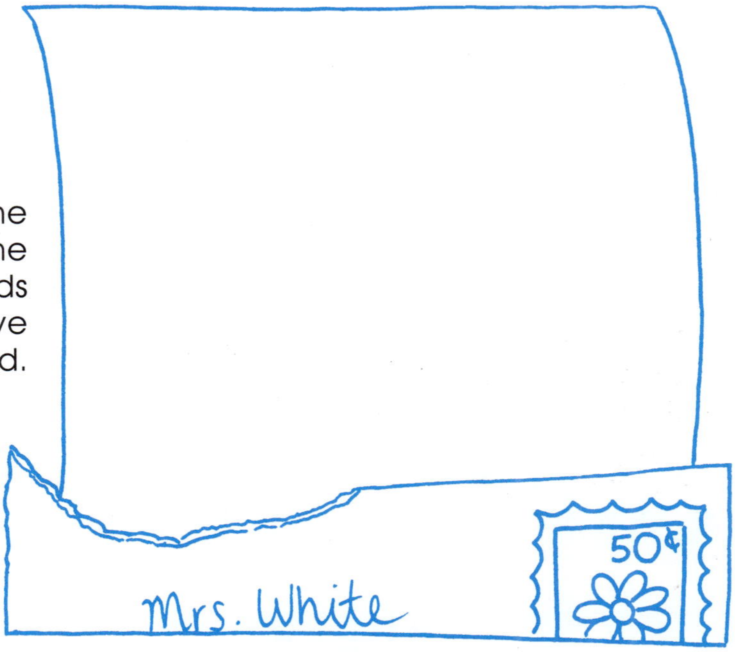

or   o + r = or

word list: for   fork   horn   short   sport   morning   horse   port   sort
word   work   sword   born

Add s, ed or ing to the following words:

sport   _____   _____

fork   _____

sort   _____   _____   _____

Using any two words from the list write your own sentence.

_____

_____

Fill in the missing word list:

You eat with a _____.

A car has one _____.

If you are not tall you are _____.

You have breakfast in the _____.

A foal is a baby _____.

Ships arrive at a _____.

Were you _____ in a hospital?

Write in the horse all the or words you have learned.

Find the words from the word list.

F	A	O	Y	U	M	C	K	Y	S	N	Z
N	K	W	U	D	O	S	M	W	P	M	P
D	W	O	R	K	R	K	B	Q	O	W	F
S	H	O	R	T	N	I	O	M	R	Q	I
S	O	K	S	O	I	O	R	B	T	Z	E
W	R	C	X	S	N	W	N	E	T	P	M
O	N	Z	D	O	G	B	O	W	O	R	D
R	K	D	S	R	F	A	Y	T	P	Z	G
D	H	O	L	T	O	S	X	H	O	W	F
K	E	O	R	L	R	X	J	V	R	F	O
K	E	R	R	Y	K	A	K	Q	T	V	R
O	Y	K	K	S	N	O	I	X	R	S	F
C	K	P	I	S	E	W	T	C	V	Z	Q

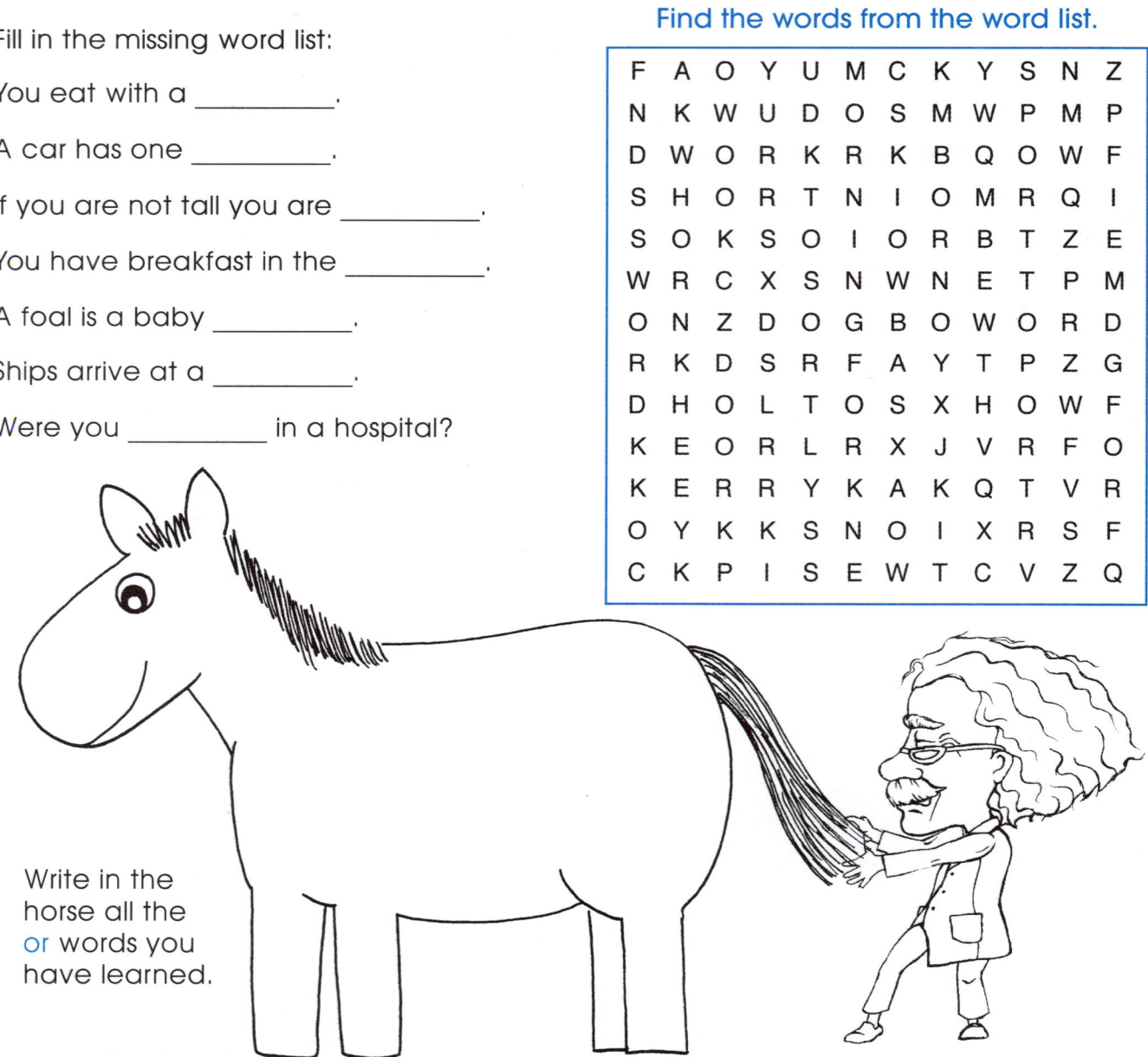

OW   o + w = ow

word list: cow   now   bow   brown   grown   frown   town   clown   down
crown   flower   owl   growl

Which list words mean:

The funniest person at the circus? _____.

An animal that says moo? _____.

The colour of chocolate? _____.

For mum on Mother's Day? _____.

I am wise and live in a tree? _____.

The opposite to up? _____.

This very moment? _____.

A fun **ow**
tongue twister.

How now brown cow
How now brown cow
How now brown cow
How now how now
Brown cow brown cow
How now brown cow
How now brown cow

Add the ow to these words:

c _ _   f r _ _ n   t _ _ n   b r _ _ n   d _ _ n   n _ _

Find the opposite to these words:

Smile _____.   Up _____.   Then _____.

Write inside the town all the ow
words you have learned.

Draw a clown with a frown on a brown cow:

aw   a + w = aw

word list: saw   draw   paw   lawn   law   straw   claw   crawl   jaw
yawn   dawn   awful

Put the words from the list in alphabetical order:

1 _____   2 _____   3 _____

4 _____   5 _____   6 _____

7 _____   8 _____   9 _____

10 _____   11 _____   12 _____

Which list words rhyme with:

saw   lawn

_____   _____

_____   _____

_____   _____

Write a sentence using at least two words from the list:

_____

_____

Draw:

When I yawn, my jaw drops.

She sat on the lawn at dawn.

Write inside the glass all the aw words you have learned.

12

ay   a + y = ay

Which list words fit these sentences?
play, way, clay

I know the _____ to school.

We can _____ at recess time.

You can make things using _____.

Circle the smaller word inside these words:

play   pray   today

_____   _____   _____

write the small word underneath.

Days of the week all have ay in them.

Sunday
Monday
Tuesday
Wednesday
Thursday
Friday
Saturday

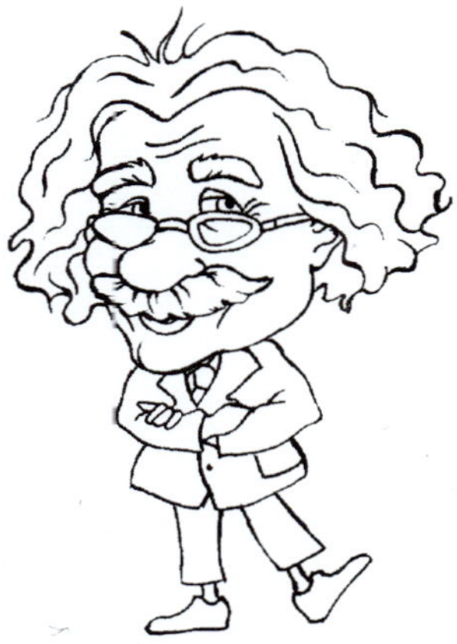

Add endings to these words: add s   add ed   add ing

play: _____   _____   _____

stay: _____   _____   _____

pray: _____   _____   _____

pay: _____   _____

Find the words from the word list.

M	C	Y	I	B	G	D	J	R	A	E	T
T	I	D	S	T	I	T	B	H	A	Y	W
D	A	A	T	V	N	O	R	J	H	O	E
Q	W	Y	A	N	P	D	A	V	V	Z	A
K	A	X	Y	Y	T	A	F	J	J	N	Z
V	Y	D	I	B	F	Y	U	V	B	P	E
M	C	L	A	Y	F	A	I	D	T	C	H
A	D	P	Q	F	C	P	M	K	O	M	P
H	F	P	R	B	P	F	Q	M	L	F	H
L	Y	U	S	A	E	A	X	A	C	Y	M
O	L	G	T	A	Y	F	Y	V	G	W	W
S	G	T	M	J	Y	D	R	C	M	A	T
D	G	V	H	Z	Z	A	U	K	X	Y	F

Write inside the haystack all the ay words you have learned.

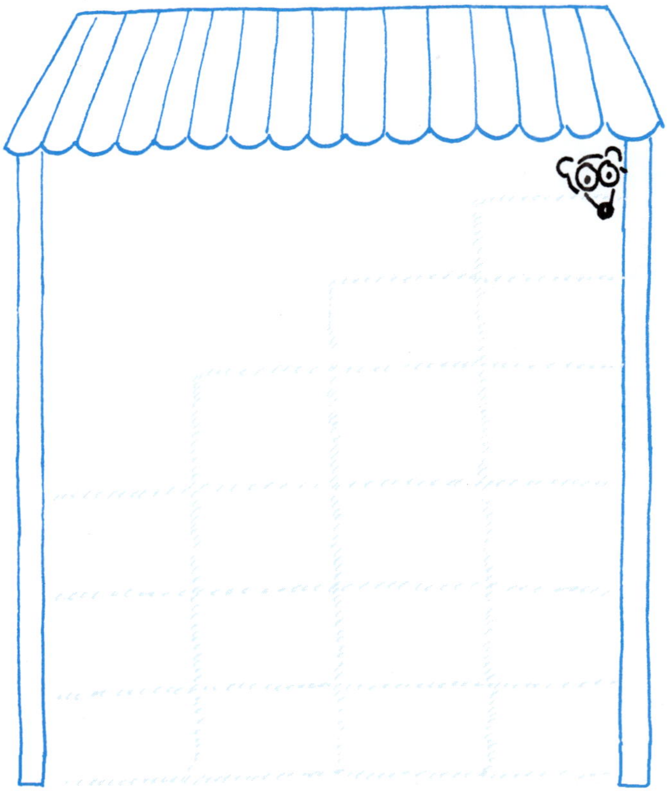

13

y on the end of a short word says i

Which list words are shown in these pictures:

_____   _____   _____

Write sentences using the words: why. spy, by

_____

_____

From the word list write what you believe
the answer should be.

Belongs to me.   _____

Next to.   _____

Mum likes to __?__ chips.   _____

Peter Pan could __?__ .   _____

A pig lives in a __?__ .   _____

I __?__ with my little eye. _____

Write inside the fly all the short y words you
have learned.

14

y on the end of a long word says e

word list: jelly   funny   sunny   bunny   happy   silly   jetty   smelly   spy   sky

Draw a happy bunny sitting on a jetty on a sunny day.

Write sentences using these words: funny, jelly, silly

_____

_____

_____

Which word within the list means:

Not sad _____.

Wobbles on a plate _____.

You can sit on it to fish _____.

Write in the sunny face all the long y words you have learned.

15

ai   a + i = ai

From the word list choose the best fit:
stain, hail, train, paint, main, rain

A _____ runs on tracks.

I love to hear the _____ on the roof.

_____ is frozen rain.

She is the _____ character in the movie.

We had to _____ over the _____ .

Professor Mentor asks, 'Which words from the word list fit into these shapes?'

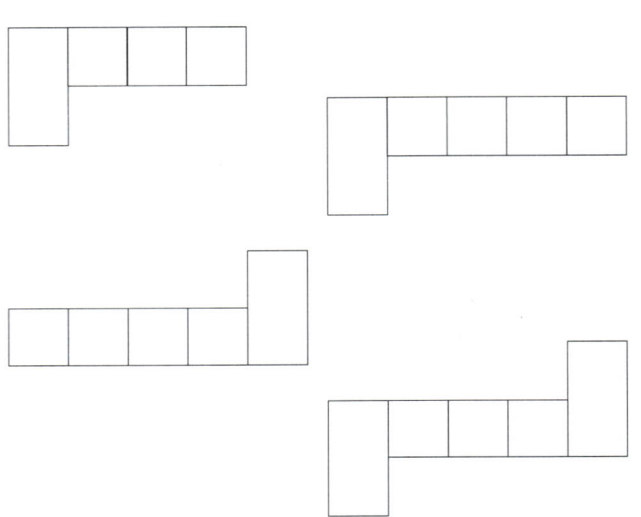

Write your own sentences including these words.
main, gain, vain, grain, plain, chain
Understand: not all words with ai sound the same.

Find the words from the word list.

V	J	H	Z	G	R	A	I	N	H	O	P
D	O	P	N	Q	H	C	F	U	K	T	M
W	A	M	U	S	N	A	I	L	F	R	W
X	Z	O	H	U	H	W	F	I	W	A	M
M	H	A	I	L	P	Q	E	W	P	I	T
F	T	P	C	B	M	R	A	E	Q	N	L
M	M	A	I	N	W	O	M	P	D	N	G
S	G	R	P	R	Q	O	U	R	I	D	X
F	S	P	A	A	N	K	E	A	E	C	K
T	W	A	I	I	S	R	T	G	R	Y	U
L	Z	I	N	L	Q	S	H	R	A	M	I
P	P	N	T	J	V	N	N	Z	I	I	Y
K	S	R	D	F	T	G	K	Y	N	G	R

ck   c + k = ck

word list: back pack sack rack lick sick rock sock luck truck

a e i o u after the vowels comes double c (ck)

Which list word means:

Opposite to front __________.

To wear on your foot __________.

It is fun to __________ icecream.

Nick's clock goes tick, tock in the back of his truck.

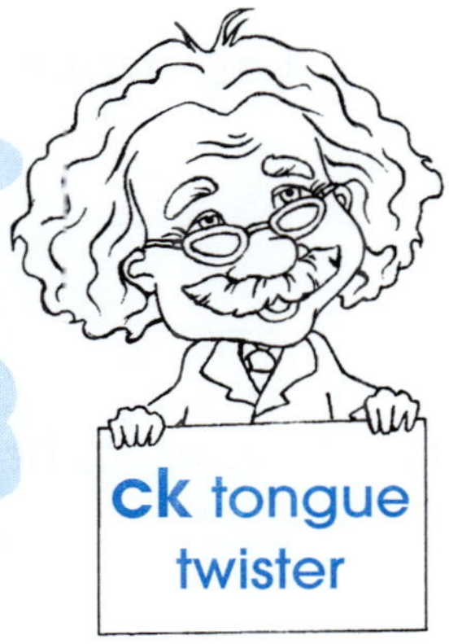

ck tongue twister

Try to use more than one of the list words in a sentence:

____

____

____

Draw a picture for each of these words:

rock	sock	truck

Funny rhyme
Chuck the Duck
drove a truck
into muck
and said
"Quack Quack"

Create you own funny rhyme with words ending with ck

____

____

____

____

____

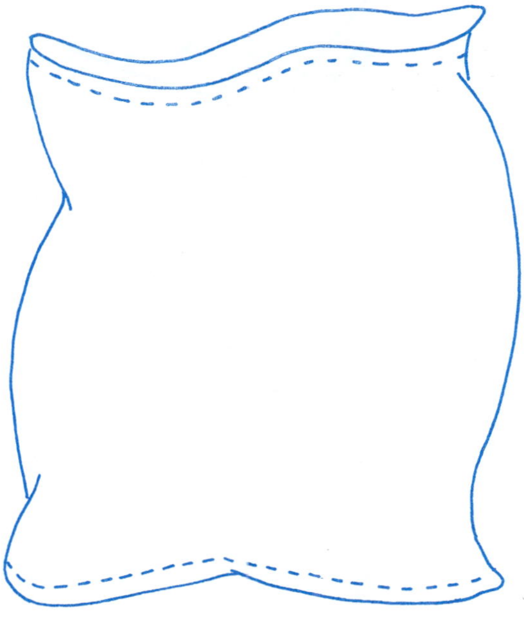

Write inside the sack all the ck words you have learned.

ea   e + a = say ea

Write these words in alphabetical order.

1 _____   2 _____   3 _____   4 _____   5 _____

6 _____   7 _____   8 _____   9 _____   10 _____

Which word fits here?

p _ _ _ s _   d _ _ _ m   _ h _ _ t

Find the words from the word list.

dream time

ea ea ea ea ea

L	G	W	B	P	Y	Q	L	V	D	O	M
V	T	N	D	T	L	S	L	A	U	J	E
Q	Q	X	E	J	D	E	E	B	Q	Z	A
H	T	J	L	A	Y	L	A	I	Y	N	T
S	T	J	C	D	T	M	F	S	U	Z	Z
U	T	W	L	K	L	U	T	F	E	A	W
Q	K	O	E	J	U	W	Z	E	B	Z	D
O	S	V	A	Z	Z	H	O	U	P	V	T
S	E	V	N	B	T	E	U	W	F	M	M
O	L	R	C	C	D	A	B	H	W	G	K
E	Y	X	Q	R	D	T	Y	E	T	F	N
Q	M	I	W	E	S	R	P	A	K	V	F
C	Q	R	E	A	D	C	E	T	T	S	O
W	J	M	Q	M	B	Q	Z	A	G	J	N
G	C	R	N	Q	X	R	Q	M	M	C	Q

Write inside the leaf all the ea words you have learned.

oo   o + o = says oo

word list: soon   spoon   moon   broom   roof   tooth   food   hoop   zoo

Write sentences using these words: spoon, roof, tooth

_____

_____

_____

Draw a picture of a spoon in a hoop under the moon.

Write inside the tooth all the oo words you have learned.

Q: What was the time when the boy went to the dentist?

A: 2.30 (tooth-hurty)

Add the oo sound and rewrite.

S _ _ n   _____

r _ _ f   _____

z _ _   _____

b r _ _ m   _____

Compound Words

A compound word is two words joined together to make a new word.

word list:	cupboard	icecream	football	weekend	bedroom	rainbow
	postcard	outback	grandfather	seagull		

Write the compound words.

cup	ball	
ice	bow	_____
foot	card	_____
week	back	_____
bed	board	cupboard
rain	father	_____
post	room	_____
out	gull	_____
grand	cream	_____
sea	end	_____

ice + cream = icecream

Write the word. Draw the picture

[rain] + [bow] = _____

[cup] + [board] = _____

[foot] + [ball] = _____

Write other compound words:

_____

_____

Homophones

Homophones are words which sound the same but are spelt differently.

word list: hear/here   bean/been   there/their/they're   flower/flour   saw/sore

Circle the correct word in these sentences, and write the corrected sentence below.

I have been/bean to the beach.

Come here/hear and here/hear this sound.

She had a saw/sore leg.

He looked over there/their.

Bread is made from flower/flour.

Grandma planted a been/bean seed.

Dad saw/sore a flower/flour.

There/they're coming to the party with they're/their friends

Find the words from the word list.

Q	T	V	R	T	H	E	I	R	D	B	Z
Z	O	H	E	R	E	S	P	B	H	G	G
U	V	P	F	C	J	A	M	H	E	A	I
A	F	A	A	N	B	W	M	B	A	Q	K
U	L	R	B	Z	E	R	P	Q	R	A	T
Q	O	X	B	C	A	G	T	C	D	Y	E
D	U	B	R	B	N	S	E	V	K	R	K
U	R	R	E	X	E	E	J	K	O	N	M
K	U	D	U	E	T	H	O	S	N	T	U
H	T	C	Q	N	N	H	F	V	H	E	F
G	H	A	D	M	J	V	E	L	U	P	M
G	E	Q	F	J	Z	T	Y	Y	M	G	C
U	R	N	O	S	E	D	L	X	R	N	E
G	E	F	F	L	O	W	E	R	C	E	Z
J	Q	M	F	L	A	Q	C	Q	R	S	R

Draw a picture:

A pretty flower

A bag of flour

Contractions

A contraction is two words shortened into one when an apostrophe replaces the missing letter or letters.

I will I'll

I am _____

They are _____

could not _____

She will _____

we are _____

I can't see

Here are the contractions. Write the two words which make them.

He's _____ _____

Don't _____ _____

She'll _____ _____

Didn't _____ _____

She's _____ _____

He'll _____ _____

Fill in the missing list word:
couldn't, don't, they're, he'll

I _____ like spinach.

_____ be happy if we go to his party.

_____ so sick they _____ go.

Rewrite these sentences using the correct contraction.

She will tell them that they can not go.

_____

_____

I did not know that he was coming too.

_____

_____

He could not open the door so we will have to use the window.

_____

_____

Draw: I'm king of the castle.

Write in the cloud all the contractions from the word list.

22

Beginning consonant blends

Read these words out loud.

bl	cl	fl	gl	sl

bl	blow	black	blue
cl	clap	close	clear
fl	flag	fly	flat
gl	glad	glitter	glow
pl	play	plain	please
sl	slow	slide	slope

Fill in the missing blends:

_ _ _ _ _ a i n   _ _ _ _ _ a t

_ _ _ _ _ o w   _ _ _ _ _ a d

_ _ _ _ _ o s e

Use each of these words in sentences: blue, clear, flag, glitter, play, slope

_____

_____

_____

_____

_____

Write the list word for these pictures.

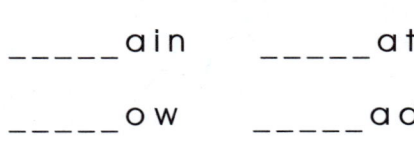

Write on the flag the beginning consonant blends.

sh sk sm sn sp st sw

sh	ship	~~shell~~	show
sk	~~skip~~	~~skim~~	sky
sm	~~small~~	~~smile~~	~~smart~~
sn	snow	~~snap~~	snake
sp	spot	~~spider~~	~~spade~~
sw	~~swim~~	~~swan~~	swing

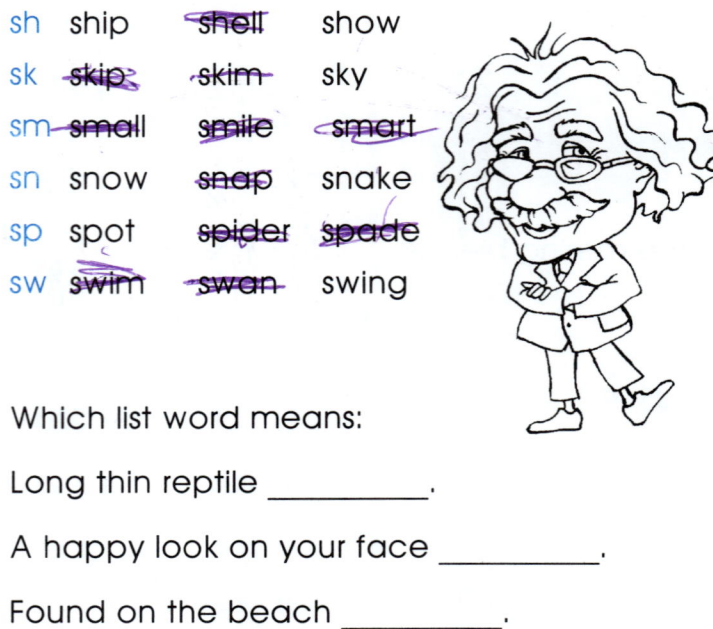

Find the words from the word list.

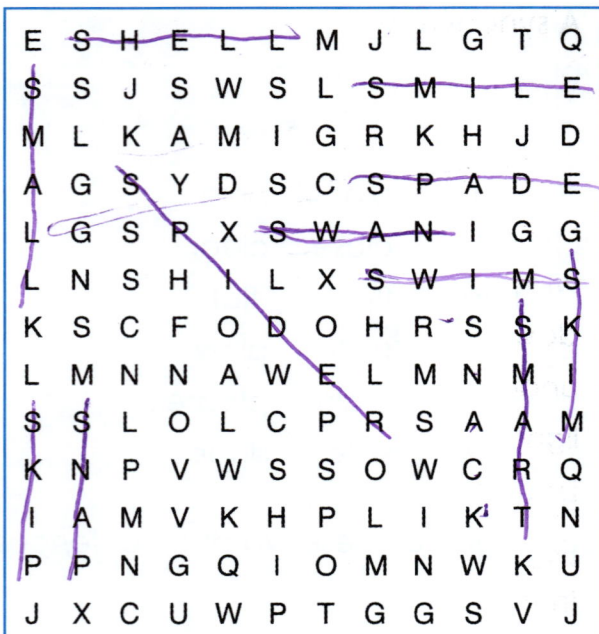

```
E S H E L L M J L G T Q
S S J S W S L S M I L E
M L K A M I G R K H J D
A G S Y D S C S P A D E
L G S P X S W A N I G G
L N S H I L X S W I M S
K S C F O D O H R S S K
L M N N A W E L M N M I
S S L O L C P R S A A M
K N P V W S S O W C R Q
I A M V K H P L I K T N
P P N G Q I O M N W K U
J X C U W P T G G S V J
```

Which list word means:

Long thin reptile _____ .

A happy look on your face _____ .

Found on the beach _____ .

Draw a picture.

Spider spinning a web

Skipping under a blue sky

A swan swimming on a pond

Professor Mentor asks, 'Which words from the word list fit into these shapes?'

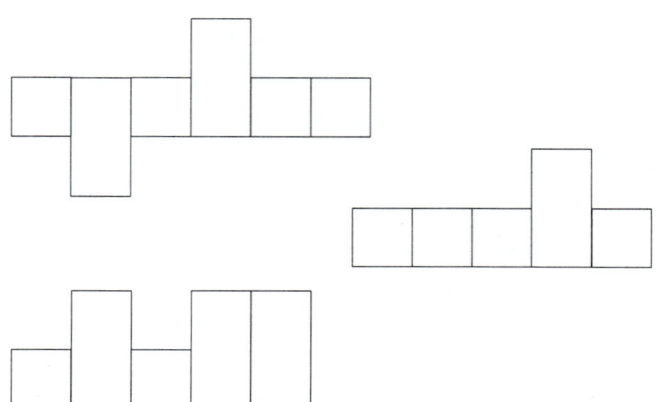

Write inside the shell all the beginning consonant blends.

Antonyms and synonyms

An antonym is a word having an opposite meaning

A synonym is a word having similar meaning

Write the antonym for these words and find them in the wordsearch.

short   _____

black   _____

wide   _____

down   _____

under   _____

light   _____

beginning _____

A	P	I	Z	A	P	V	S	A	L	Y	U
P	K	Z	G	D	Y	N	T	S	P	J	J
X	D	A	R	K	Y	A	K	A	K	O	X
Q	V	H	X	V	I	M	P	N	L	D	V
V	U	I	O	M	V	E	U	W	D	L	W
V	Y	N	E	J	F	K	O	A	J	I	L
A	Y	A	Y	P	J	V	Q	R	W	Q	B
S	X	R	Z	N	Y	V	G	F	F	H	Z
H	L	R	T	E	O	P	N	E	Y	O	G
S	J	O	W	Z	A	M	B	N	N	L	A
H	C	W	B	U	P	I	Q	S	I	D	O
K	Z	V	E	F	F	M	W	N	R	O	Q
K	P	I	G	V	W	H	I	T	E	V	G
M	Z	C	O	B	H	Y	L	Z	R	E	B
L	E	D	P	F	G	E	H	E	G	R	B

Find the synonyms for the word in brackets in these sentences: wet, broke, safe, edge

She felt [alright] at home. _____

It was a cold and [damp] night. _____

We planted flowers around the [border]. _____

The cup [smashed] when it was dropped. _____

Choose two antonyms and two synonyms and draw them.

Practise writing these sentences: An antonym is a word having the opposite meaning.

_____

_____

A synonym is a word having a similar meaning.

_____

_____

Consonant blend endings   nd ng nk nt

Place from the list, word in these sentences:
drink, song, went, front, stand, ring

I _____ to the shop to have a _____.

He can _____ at the _____ of the line.

Listen to the radio station

for your favourite _____.

Write any words which rhyme with these list words:

Sand _____ _____ _____.

Ring _____ _____ _____.

Went _____ _____ _____.

Draw a plate on a stand.

Find the words from the word list.

```
W E N T D S K K N A F L
A I S E I E N E N A R A
I N N F A R S D N K O B
H N R K T H E B A N N A
A H R N I N G N N T T N
N T E N T N N B H N W K
G D H T E H A G N H H S
D R I N K S T H I N K A
A P L A N T R I N G O N
B E N D T A R S S A N D
H N N N E N B N S O N G
D K B K O D K N D A N A
D N H A P L K A H E L N
```

Write inside the think balloon blend words you have learned.

Professor Mentor says. — 'Now you have learnt all these words it's time to ask an adult to help you with testing.'

Learning to Spell

Look   Look carefully at the word
Say   Say the word out loud
Cover Cover the word
Write Write the word
Check Check your spelling of the word

L S C W C	TEST YOURSELF	ADULT TEST	L S C W C	TEST YOURSELF	ADULT TEST
and			down		
in			play		
one			away		
not			jump		
the			where		
blue			for		
go			me		
two			my		
help			broom		
make			we		
big			find		
is			said		
a			funny		
red			little		
to			yellow		
come			all		
look			do		
you			so		
here			eat		
three			our		
can			with		
it			now		
I			soon		
run			get		
up			spoon		

L S C W C	TEST YOURSELF	ADULT TEST	L S C W C	TEST YOURSELF	ADULT TEST
I'll			brown		
good			like		
pretty			after		
as			fly		
over			some		
give			has		
am			be		
he			saw		
can't			did		
into			no		
too			will		
yes			came		
out			ran		
they're			who		
must			they		
well			couldn't		
black			four		
have			please		
we'll			again		
by			of		
round			take		
had			how		
are			may		
on			then		
but			giving		
new			live		
was			an		
at			her		
ride			once		
want			around		
there			fast		
went			sit		

L S C W C	TEST YOURSELF	ADULT TEST	L S C W C	TEST YOURSELF	ADULT TEST
don't			five		
green			before		
tell			gave		
its			read		
or			both		
very			many		
us			those		
stop			call		
he's			wash		
him			them		
open			ask		
could			let		
his			were		
put			from		
because			old		
first			always		
sleep			does		
found			sing		
pull			best		
their			goes		
made			right		
these			buy		
would			off		
use			upon		
she'll			cold		
any			which		
just			why		
walk			your		
every			carry		
know			draw		
when			far		
been			hold		

L S C W C	TEST YOURSELF	ADULT TEST	L S C W C	TEST YOURSELF	ADULT TEST
keep			both		
long			moth		
only			thing		
shall			green		
quiche			question		
try			dinner		
wheel			letter		
about			fern		
clean			fork		
drink			horn		
full			morning		
hot			brown		
kind			town		
much			down		
own			draw		
show			paw		
ten			lawn		
warm			clay		
work			away		
better			today		
cut			dry		
eight			spy		
got			sky		
hurt			funny		
white			sunny		
shop			jetty		
cheese			pull		
children			their		
farm			made		
party			these		
card			would		
bark			use		

L S C W C	TEST YOURSELF	ADULT TEST	L S C W C	TEST YOURSELF	ADULT TEST
snail			cold		
any			luck		
just			truck		
walk			your		
every			carry		
know			draw		
rack			far		
been			hold		
five			keep		
before			long		
gave			only		
read			shall		
both			clean		
many			try		
those			dream		
call			about		
wash			clean		
them			drink		
ask			full		
let			hot		
were			kind		
from			much		
old			own		
always			show		
does			ten		
sing			warm		
best			work		
goes			better		
right			cut		
buy			eight		
off			got		
upon			hurt		

L S C W C	TEST YOURSELF	ADULT TEST	L S C W C	TEST YOURSELF	ADULT TEST
laugh			say		
myself			see		
pick			tree		
six			three		
today			knee		
ate			bee		
write			week		
bring			green		
done			feet		
fall			sweet		
grow			sheet		
if			keep		
light			sleep		
never			sheep		
seven			weed		
small			feed		
together					

Maths

2 times table

Trace over the number in the box

1	x	2	=	2
2	x	2	=	4
3	x	2	=	6
4	x	2	=	8
5	x	2	=	10
6	x	2	=	12
7	x	2	=	14
8	x	2	=	16
9	x	2	=	18
10	x	2	=	20
11	x	2	=	22
12	x	2	=	24

2	÷	2	=	1
4	÷	2	=	2
6	÷	2	=	3
8	÷	2	=	4
10	÷	2	=	5
12	÷	2	=	6
14	÷	2	=	7
16	÷	2	=	8
18	÷	2	=	9
20	÷	2	=	10
22	÷	2	=	11
24	÷	2	=	12

Multiplication grid by 2

X	1	2	3	4	5	6	7	8	9	10	11	12
2	2											

Colour the squares below that are multiples of 2

1	2	3	4	5	6	7	8	9	10
11	12	13	14	15	16	17	18	19	20
21	22	23	24	25	26	27	28	29	30
31	32	33	34	35	36	37	38	39	40
41	42	43	44	45	46	47	48	49	50

Which number comes next?

1. 2 4 ☐ 8 10 ☐
2. 20 18 ☐ 14 ☐ 10
3. 36 38 40 ☐ 44 ☐
4. 1 3 ☐ ☐ 9 ☐
5. 41 43 45 ☐ 49 ☐

Number facts

$5 + 2 =$ $2 + 5 =$
$7 - 5 =$ $7 - 2 =$
$12 + 2 =$ $2 + 12 =$
$14 - 12 =$ $14 - 2 =$
$2 + 9 =$ $9 + 2 =$
$21 - 2 =$ $21 - 19 =$

Time challenge

Start _____ Finish _____ Time taken _____

1. $2 + 5 =$
2. $9 + 2 =$
3. $20 - 2 =$
4. $6 \times 2 =$
5. $46 - 2 =$
6. $24 \div 2 =$
7. $17 - 2 =$
8. $2 \times 11 =$
9. $8 \div 2 =$
10. $2 + 13 =$

Start _____ Finish _____ Time taken _____

11. $5 \times 2 =$
12. $3 \times 2 =$
13. $7 \times 2 =$
14. $10 \times 2 =$
15. $4 \times 2 =$
16. $9 \times 2 =$
17. $6 \times 2 =$
18. $8 \times 2 =$
19. $2 \times 2 =$
20. $11 \times 2 =$

Maths words

1. 5 more than 2 =
2. 2 times 7 =
3. how many 2's in 6? =
4. 14 minus 2 =
5. 6 lots of 2 =
6. 8 lots of 2 =
7. 11 plus 2 =
8. 8 and 2 =
9. 2 and 2 and 2 =
10. 2 more than 23 =

How many?

24 socks hanging on a line.
How many pairs? _____
Colour the socks in pairs.

3 times table

Trace over the number in the box

1 x 3 =	3	3 ÷ 3 =	1
2 x 3 =	6	6 ÷ 3 =	2
3 x 3 =	9	9 ÷ 3 =	3
4 x 3 =	12	12 ÷ 3 =	4
5 x 3 =	15	15 ÷ 3 =	5
6 x 3 =	18	18 ÷ 3 =	6
7 x 3 =	21	21 ÷ 3 =	7
8 x 3 =	24	24 ÷ 3 =	8
9 x 3 =	27	27 ÷ 3 =	9
10 x 3 =	30	30 ÷ 3 =	10
11 x 3 =	33	33 ÷ 3 =	11
12 x 3 =	36	36 ÷ 3 =	12

Multiplication grid by 3

X	1	2	3	4	5	6	7	8	9	10	11	12
3						18						

Colour the squares below that are multiples of 3

21	22	23	24	25	26	27	28	29	30
31	32	33	34	35	36	37	38	39	40
41	42	43	44	45	46	47	48	49	50
51	52	53	54	55	56	57	58	59	60
61	62	63	64	65	66	67	68	69	70

Which number comes next?

1. 3 ☐ 9 ☐ 15 18
2. 30 33 ☐ ☐ ☐
3. 24 21 ☐ ☐ 12
4. 2 5 ☐ 11 ☐
5. 39 ☐ 33 ☐

Number facts

6 + 3 = _____   3 + 6 = _____
15 − 3 = _____   15 − 12 = _____
3 + 11 = _____   11 + 3 = _____
4 x 3 = _____   3 x 4 = _____
21 − 3 = _____   21 − 18 = _____

Time challenge

Start _____   Finish _____   Time taken _____   Start _____   Finish _____   Time taken _____

1. 3 + 8 = _____
2. 3 x 3 = _____
3. 16 − 3 = _____
4. 18 ÷ 3 = _____
5. 9 − 3 = _____
6. 3 + 14 = _____
7. 5 + 3 = _____
8. 12 ÷ 3 = _____
9. 8 − 3 = _____
10. 2 + 13 = _____

11. 3 x 3 = _____
12. 11 x 3 = _____
13. 2 x 3 = _____
14. 6 x 3 = _____
15. 4 x 3 = _____
16. 8 x 3 = _____
17. 12 x 3 = _____
18. 5 x 3 = _____
19. 10 x 3 = _____
20. 7 x 3 = _____

Maths words

1. how many 3's in 9? = _____
2. 19 − 3 = _____
3. 6 more than 3 = _____
4. 15 take away 3 = _____
5. 2 plus 3 = _____
6. 3 times 4 = _____
7. 3 and 3 and 3 = _____
8. 7 lots of 3 = _____
9. 8 more than 26 = _____
10. 8 and 3 = _____

How many?

How many balloons? _____
How many groups of 3? _____
Colour the balloons.

4 times table

Trace over the number in the box

1	x	4	=	4
2	x	4	=	8
3	x	4	=	12
4	x	4	=	16
5	x	4	=	20
6	x	4	=	24
7	x	4	=	28
8	x	4	=	32
9	x	4	=	36
10	x	4	=	40
11	x	4	=	44
12	x	4	=	48

4	÷	4	=	1
8	÷	4	=	2
12	÷	4	=	3
16	÷	4	=	4
20	÷	4	=	5
24	÷	4	=	6
28	÷	4	=	7
32	÷	4	=	8
36	÷	4	=	9
40	÷	4	=	10
44	÷	4	=	11
48	÷	4	=	12

Multiplication grid by 4

X	1	2	3	4	5	6	7	8	9	10	11	12
4				16					36			

Colour the squares below that are multiples of 4

41	42	43	44	45	46	47	48	49	50
51	52	53	54	55	56	57	58	59	60
61	62	63	64	65	66	67	68	69	70
71	72	73	74	75	76	77	78	79	80
81	82	83	84	85	86	87	88	89	90

Which number comes next?

1. 8 12 ☐ 20 ☐
2. 48 44 ☐ ☐ 32
3. 33 37 41 ☐ ☐
4. 62 58 ☐ 50 ☐
5. 1 5 ☐ 13 ☐

Number facts

$4 + 6 =$ $6 + 4 =$
$5 \times 4 =$ $4 \times 5 =$
$17 - 4 =$ $17 - 13 =$
$9 + 4 =$ $4 + 9 =$
$3 \times 4 =$ $4 \times 3 =$

Time challenge

Start ____ Finish ____ Time taken ____

1. $4 - 2 =$
2. $12 \div 4 =$
3. $2 \times 4 =$
4. $4 + 13 =$
5. $6 + 4 =$
6. $18 - 4 =$
7. $4 \times 7 =$
8. $20 \div 4 =$
9. $27 - 4 =$
10. $9 + 4 =$

Start ____ Finish ____ Time taken ____

11. $3 \times 4 =$
12. $6 \times 4 =$
13. $7 \times 4 =$
14. $4 \times 4 =$
15. $2 \times 4 =$
16. $8 \times 4 =$
17. $9 \times 4 =$
18. $10 \times 4 =$
19. $11 \times 4 =$
20. $5 \times 4 =$

Maths words

1. 16 minus 4 =
2. 4 and 4 and 4 =
3. 6 lots of 4 =
4. 4 more than 7 =
5. how many 4's in 16 =
6. 13 and 4 =
7. 5 times 4 =
8. 17 plus 4 =
9. 25 take away 4 =
10. 4 more than 29 =

How many Tens and Units

1. 45 = ____ tens and ____ units
2. 39 = ____ tens and ____ units
3. 12 = ____ tens and ____ units
4. 100 = ____ tens and ____ units
5. 3 = ____ tens and ____ units

5 times table

Trace over the number in the box

1 x 5 =	5
2 x 5 =	10
3 x 5 =	15
4 x 5 =	20
5 x 5 =	25
6 x 5 =	30
7 x 5 =	35
8 x 5 =	40
9 x 5 =	45
10 x 5 =	50
11 x 5 =	55
12 x 5 =	60

5 ÷ 5 =	1
10 ÷ 5 =	2
15 ÷ 5 =	3
20 ÷ 5 =	4
25 ÷ 5 =	5
30 ÷ 5 =	6
35 ÷ 5 =	7
40 ÷ 5 =	8
45 ÷ 5 =	9
50 ÷ 5 =	10
55 ÷ 5 =	11
60 ÷ 5 =	12

5 is an odd number.

Colour the five

Multiplication grid by 5

X	1	2	3	4	5	6	7	8	9	10	11	12
5					25	30				50		

Colour the squares below that are multiples of 5

31	32	33	34	35	36	37	38	39	40
41	42	43	44	45	46	47	48	49	50
51	52	53	54	55	56	57	58	59	60
61	62	63	64	65	66	67	68	69	70
71	72	73	74	75	76	77	78	79	80

Which number comes next?

1. 10 15 ☐ 25 30
2. 65 60 ☐ ☐ 45
3. 2 7 ☐ 17 ☐ ☐
4. 53 48 ☐ 38 ☐
5. 35 ☐ 45 ☐ ☐

Number facts

$5 + 10 =$ $10 + 5 =$
$6 \times 5 =$ $5 \times 6 =$
$18 - 5 =$ $18 - 13 =$
$13 + 5 =$ $5 + 13 =$
$5 \times 9 =$ $9 \times 5 =$

Time challenge

Start ____ Finish ____ Time taken ____   Start ____ Finish ____ Time taken ____

1. $25 \div 5 =$
2. $5 + 10 =$
3. $2 \times 5 =$
4. $17 - 5 =$
5. $24 + 5 =$
6. $40 \div 5 =$
7. $5 \times 9 =$
8. $5 + 31 =$
9. $26 - 5 =$
10. $12 \times 5 =$

11. $4 \times 5 =$
12. $8 \times 5 =$
13. $5 \times 5 =$
14. $7 \times 5 =$
15. $11 \times 5 =$
16. $3 \times 5 =$
17. $9 \times 5 =$
18. $6 \times 5 =$
19. $12 \times 5 =$
20. $2 \times 5 =$

Maths words

1. 3 lots of 5 =
2. how many 5's in 45? =
3. 18 plus 5 =
4. 5 and 5 and 5 =
5. 6 times 5 =
6. 7 and 5 =
7. 5 more than 9 =
8. 34 plus 5 =
9. 14 take away 5 =
10. 2 times 5 =

Watch the sign

1. $10 + 6 =$
2. $5 \times 3 =$
3. $19 - 2 =$
4. $12 \times 2 =$
5. $25 + 25 =$
6. $5 + 5 + 5 =$
7. $25 \div 5 =$
8. $20 - 15 =$
9. $15 - 15 =$

6 times table

Trace over the number in the box

1 x 6 =	6	6 ÷ 6 =	1
2 x 6 =	12	12 ÷ 6 =	2
3 x 6 =	18	18 ÷ 6 =	3
4 x 6 =	24	24 ÷ 6 =	4
5 x 6 =	30	30 ÷ 6 =	5
6 x 6 =	36	36 ÷ 6 =	6
7 x 6 =	42	42 ÷ 6 =	7
8 x 6 =	48	48 ÷ 6 =	8
9 x 6 =	54	54 ÷ 6 =	9
10 x 6 =	60	60 ÷ 6 =	10
11 x 6 =	66	66 ÷ 6 =	11
12 x 6 =	72	72 ÷ 6 =	12

Multiplication grid by 6

X	1	2	3	4	5	6	7	8	9	10	11	12
6	6			24						60		

Colour the squares below that are multiples of 6

51	52	53	54	55	56	57	58	59	60
61	62	63	64	65	66	67	68	69	70
71	72	73	74	75	76	77	78	79	80
81	82	83	84	85	86	87	88	89	90
91	92	93	94	95	96	97	98	99	100

Which number comes next?

1. 18 24 ☐ 36 ☐
2. 60 54 ☐ 42 ☐
3. 4 10 ☐ 22 ☐
4. 37 31 ☐ 19 ☐
5. 66 72 ☐ 84 ☐

Number facts

6 x 2 = ___   2 x 6 = ___
15 + 6 = ___   6 + 15 = ___
21 – 6 = ___   21 – 15 = ___
8 x 6 = ___   6 x 8 = ___
6 + 24 = ___   24 + 6 = ___

Time challenge

Start ___ Finish ___ Time taken ___   Start ___ Finish ___ Time taken ___

1. 66 ÷ 6 = ___   11. 4 x 6 = ___
2. 32 + 6 = ___   12. 7 x 6 = ___
3. 6 x 7 = ___   13. 12 x 6 = ___
4. 15 – 6 = ___   14. 9 x 6 = ___
5. 30 ÷ 6 = ___   15. 2 x 6 = ___
6. 14 + 6 = ___   16. 8 x 6 = ___
7. 6 x 11 = ___   17. 5 x 6 = ___
8. 19 – 6 = ___   18. 11 x 6 = ___
9. 36 – 10 = ___   19. 3 x 6 = ___
10. 6 x 5 = ___   20. 6 x 6 = ___

Maths words

1. 18 take away 6 = ___
2. 6 plus 13 = ___
3. 5 lots of 6 = ___
4. 6 more than 15 = ___
5. 7 and 6 = ___
6. 33 minus 6 = ___
7. 6 times 8 = ___
8. 6 and 6 and 6 = ___
9. 11 and 6 = ___
10. 32 plus 6 = ___

How many?

1. minutes in 1 hour? ___
2. days in 1 week? ___
3. hours in 1 day? ___
4. months in 1 year ___
5. months in summer? ___

7 times table

Trace over the number in the box

1	x	7	=	7	7	÷	7	=	1
2	x	7	=	14	14	÷	7	=	2
3	x	7	=	21	21	÷	7	=	3
4	x	7	=	28	28	÷	7	=	4
5	x	7	=	35	35	÷	7	=	5
6	x	7	=	42	42	÷	7	=	6
7	x	7	=	49	49	÷	7	=	7
8	x	7	=	56	56	÷	7	=	8
9	x	7	=	63	63	÷	7	=	9
10	x	7	=	70	70	÷	7	=	10
11	x	7	=	77	77	÷	7	=	11
12	x	7	=	84	84	÷	7	=	12

Multiplication grid by 7

X	1	2	3	4	5	6	7	8	9	10	11	12
7		14						56				

Colour the squares below that are multiples of 7

11	12	13	14	15	16	17	18	19	20
21	22	23	24	25	26	27	28	29	30
31	32	33	34	35	36	37	38	39	40
41	42	43	44	45	46	47	48	49	50
51	52	53	54	55	56	57	58	59	60

Which number comes next?

1. 0 7 ☐ 21 ☐
2. 49 42 ☐ 28 ☐
3. 16 23 ☐ 37 ☐
4. 83 76 ☐ 62 ☐
5. 32 ☐ 46 53 ☐

Number facts

$16 - 7 =$ $16 - 9 =$
$6 \times 7 =$ $7 \times 6 =$
$7 + 15 =$ $15 + 7 =$
$23 - 7 =$ $23 - 16 =$
$14 \div 7 =$ $14 \div 2 =$

Time challenge

Start _____ Finish _____ Time taken _____   Start _____ Finish _____ Time taken _____

1. $15 + 7 =$
2. $84 \div 7 =$
3. $33 - 7 =$
4. $7 \times 9 =$
5. $7 + 23 =$
6. $56 \div 7 =$
7. $12 \times 7 =$
8. $56 - 7 =$
9. $14 + 7 =$
10. $62 - 7 =$

11. $6 \times 7 =$
12. $4 \times 7 =$
13. $9 \times 7 =$
14. $3 \times 7 =$
15. $8 \times 7 =$
16. $11 \times 7 =$
17. $10 \times 7 =$
18. $5 \times 7 =$
19. $7 \times 7 =$
20. $2 \times 7 =$

Maths words

1. 7 plus 19 =
2. 14 more than 7 =
3. 7 times 3 =
4. 7 and 7 and 7 =
5. 22 take away 7 =
6. 7 and 13 =
7. 41 plus 7 =
8. 7 lots of 9 =
9. 14 minus 7 =
10. how many 7's in 21? =

Colour the shapes which show halves

8 times table

Trace over the number in the box

1	x	8	=	8	8	÷	8	=	1
2	x	8	=	16	16	÷	8	=	2
3	x	8	=	24	24	÷	8	=	3
4	x	8	=	32	32	÷	8	=	4
5	x	8	=	40	40	÷	8	=	5
6	x	8	=	48	48	÷	8	=	6
7	x	8	=	56	56	÷	8	=	7
8	x	8	=	64	64	÷	8	=	8
9	x	8	=	72	72	÷	8	=	9
10	x	8	=	80	80	÷	8	=	10
11	x	8	=	88	88	÷	8	=	11
12	x	8	=	96	96	÷	8	=	12

Multiplication grid by 8

X	1	2	3	4	5	6	7	8	9	10	11	12
8							56			80		

Colour the squares below that are multiples of 8

71	72	73	74	75	76	77	78	79	80
81	82	83	84	85	86	87	88	89	90
91	92	93	94	95	96	97	98	99	100
101	102	103	104	105	106	107	108	109	110
111	112	113	114	115	116	117	118	119	120

Which number comes next?

1. 64 72 ☐ 88 ☐
2. 39 31 ☐ 15 ☐
3. 15 23 ☐ 39 ☐
4. 48 40 32 ☐ ☐
5. 2 ☐ 18 ☐ 34

Number facts

8 + 7 =   7 + 8 =

32 ÷ 8 =   32 ÷ 4 =

3 x 8 =   8 x 3 =

21 − 8 =   21 − 13 =

16 + 8 =   8 + 16 =

Time challenge

Start _____ Finish _____ Time taken _____   Start _____ Finish _____ Time taken _____

1. 12 − 8 =   11. 3 x 8 =
2. 88 ÷ 8 =   12. 7 x 8 =
3. 8 + 23 =   13. 10 x 8 =
4. 8 x 7 =   14. 4 x 8 =
5. 61 − 8 =   15. 8 x 8 =
6. 96 ÷ 8 =   16. 12 x 8 =
7. 53 + 8 =   17. 6 x 8 =
8. 8 x 2 =   18. 9 x 8 =
9. 14 − 8 =   19. 2 x 8 =
10. 8 x 12 =   20. 5 x 8 =

Maths words

1. 8 more than 13 =
2. 8 times 4 =
3. 19 and 8 =
4. 12 lots of 8 =
5. 8 plus 18 =
6. 61 minus 8 =
7. how many 8's in 32 =
8. 8 more than 32 =
9. 36 take away 8 =
10. 8 and 8 and 8 =

Tuck shop specials

fruit box drink **30ᶜ**   lollipop **20ᶜ**   fresh fruit **10ᶜ**

How much would these cost?

1 fruit drink + 1 lolly pop =

3 pieces of fruit =

2 lollipops + 1 piece of fruit =

4 fruit box drinks =

1 of each item =

9 times table

Trace over the number in the box

1 x 9 =	9	9 ÷ 9 =	1
2 x 9 =	18	18 ÷ 9 =	2
3 x 9 =	27	27 ÷ 9 =	3
4 x 9 =	36	36 ÷ 9 =	4
5 x 9 =	45	45 ÷ 9 =	5
6 x 9 =	54	54 ÷ 9 =	6
7 x 9 =	63	63 ÷ 9 =	7
8 x 9 =	72	72 ÷ 9 =	8
9 x 9 =	81	81 ÷ 9 =	9
10 x 9 =	90	90 ÷ 9 =	10
11 x 9 =	99	99 ÷ 9 =	11
12 x 9 =	108	108 ÷ 9 =	12

Multiplication grid by 9

X	1	2	3	4	5	6	7	8	9	10	11	12
9				36	45							

Colour the squares below that are multiples of 9

51	52	53	54	55	56	57	58	59	60
61	62	63	64	65	66	67	68	69	70
71	72	73	74	75	76	77	78	79	80
81	82	83	84	85	86	87	88	89	90
91	92	93	94	95	96	97	98	99	100

Which number comes next?

1. 90 99 ☐ 117 ☐
2. 90 81 ☐ 63 ☐
3. 8 ☐ 26 ☐ 44
4. 53 44 ☐ 26 ☐
5. 1 ☐ 19 28 ☐

Number facts

72 ÷ 9 =   72 ÷ 8 =
4 x 9 =   9 x 4 =
33 − 9 =   33 − 24 =
9 + 17 =   17 + 9 =
9 x 8 =   8 x 9 =

Time challenge

Start _____ Finish _____ Time taken _____

1. 9 x 9 =
2. 32 − 9 =
3. 108 ÷ 9 =
4. 16 + 9 =
5. 17 − 9 =
6. 3 x 9 =
7. 54 ÷ 9 =
8. 37 − 9 =
9. 9 + 18 =
10. 9 x 5 =

Start _____ Finish _____ Time taken _____

11. 5 x 9 =
12. 8 x 9 =
13. 12 x 9 =
14. 10 x 9 =
15. 3 x 9 =
16. 6 x 9 =
17. 9 x 9 =
18. 11 x 9 =
19. 7 x 9 =
20. 4 x 9 =

Maths words

1. 9 and 9 and 9 =
2. 41 take away 9 =
3. 9 more than 15 =
4. how many 9's in 54 =
5. 13 minus 9 =
6. 9 plus 14 =
7. 8 lots of 9 =
8. 19 and 9 =
9. 6 times 9 =
10. 9 add 24 =

Watch the sign + − x

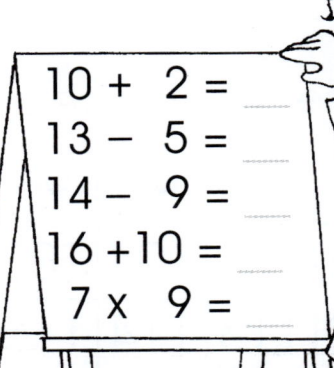

10 + 2 =
13 − 5 =
14 − 9 =
16 + 10 =
7 x 9 =

10 times table

Trace over the number in the box

1 x 10 =	10	10 ÷ 10 = 1
2 x 10 =	20	20 ÷ 10 = 2
3 x 10 =	30	30 ÷ 10 = 3
4 x 10 =	40	40 ÷ 10 = 4
5 x 10 =	50	50 ÷ 10 = 5
6 x 10 =	60	60 ÷ 10 = 6
7 x 10 =	70	70 ÷ 10 = 7
8 x 10 =	80	80 ÷ 10 = 8
9 x 10 =	90	90 ÷ 10 = 9
10 x 10 =	100	100 ÷ 10 = 10
11 x 10 =	110	110 ÷ 10 = 11
12 x 10 =	120	120 ÷ 10 = 12

Multiplication grid by 10

X	1	2	3	4	5	6	7	8	9	10	11	12
10			30						90			

Colour the squares below that are multiples of 10

91	92	93	94	95	96	97	98	99	100
101	102	103	104	105	106	107	108	109	110
111	112	113	114	115	116	117	118	119	120
121	122	123	124	125	126	127	128	129	130
131	132	133	134	135	136	137	138	139	140

Which number comes next?

1. 10 20 ☐ 40 ☐
2. 100 90 ☐ 70 ☐
3. 87 ☐ 67 57 ☐
4. 3 13 23 ☐ 43 ☐
5. 22 ☐ 42 ☐ 62

Number facts

5 × 10 =   10 × 5 =
60 ÷ 10 =   60 ÷ 6 =
41 − 10 =   41 − 31 =
10 × 8 =   8 × 10 =
65 + 10 =   10 + 65 =

Time challenge

Start ____ Finish ____ Time taken ____   Start ____ Finish ____ Time taken ____

1. 10 × 8 =
2. 53 − 10 =
3. 110 ÷ 10 =
4. 19 + 10 =
5. 69 − 10 =
6. 10 × 10 =
7. 10 ÷ 10 =
8. 120 − 10 =
9. 10 + 23 =
10. 10 × 11 =

11. 7 × 10 =
12. 4 × 10 =
13. 12 × 10 =
14. 9 × 10 =
15. 5 × 10 =
16. 8 × 10 =
17. 3 × 10 =
18. 11 × 10 =
19. 6 × 10 =
20. 2 × 10 =

Maths words

1. 17 minus 10 =
2. 9 plus 10 =
3. 6 lots of 10 =
4. 24 and 10 =
5. 10 times 8 =
6. 13 add 10 =
7. 10 and 10 and 10 =
8. 57 take away 10 =
9. 10 more than 42 =
10. how many 10's in 90 =

More or less

1. ____ is 5 more than 6
2. ____ is 2 less than 9
3. ____ is 9 more than 3
4. ____ is 4 less than 8
5. ____ is 7 more than 10
6. ____ is 11 less than 12

11 times table

Trace over the number in the box

1	x	11	=	11			
2	x	11	=	22			
3	x	11	=	33			
4	x	11	=	44			
5	x	11	=	55			
6	x	11	=	66			
7	x	11	=	77			
8	x	11	=	88			
9	x	11	=	99			
10	x	11	=	110			
11	x	11	=	121			
12	x	11	=	132			

11	÷	11	=	1
22	÷	11	=	2
33	÷	11	=	3
44	÷	11	=	4
55	÷	11	=	5
66	÷	11	=	6
77	÷	11	=	7
88	÷	11	=	8
99	÷	11	=	9
110	÷	11	=	10
121	÷	11	=	11
132	÷	11	=	12

Multiplication grid by 11

X	1	2	3	4	5	6	7	8	9	10	11	12
11			33				77				121	

Colour the squares below that are multiples of 11

61	62	63	64	65	66	67	68	69	70
71	72	73	74	75	76	77	78	79	80
81	82	83	84	85	86	87	88	89	90
91	92	93	94	95	96	97	98	99	100
101	102	103	104	105	106	107	108	109	110

Which number comes next?

1. 12 23 ☐ 45 ☐
2. 132 121 ☐ 99 88
3. 4 15 ☐ 37 ☐
4. 92 81 ☐ 59 ☐
5. 46 57 ☐ 79 ☐

Number facts

9 x 11 =   11 x 9 =
132 ÷ 11 =   132 ÷ 12 =
56 – 11 =   56 – 45 =
11 x 6 =   6 x 11 =
23 + 11 =   11 + 23 =

Time challenge

Start _____ Finish _____ Time taken _____   Start _____ Finish _____ Time taken _____

1. 11 x 9 =   11.   2 x 11 =
2. 132 ÷ 11 =   12.   6 x 11 =
3. 16 + 11 =   13.   9 x 11 =
4. 57 – 11 =   14.   3 x 11 =
5. 11 x 11 =   15.   7 x 11 =
6. 77 ÷ 11 =   16. 10 x 11 =
7. 94 – 11 =   17.   4 x 11 =
8. 18 + 11 =   18.   8 x 11 =
9. 11 + 41 =   19. 12 x 11 =
10. 12 – 11 =   20.   5 x 11 =

Maths words

1. 65 minus 11 =
2. how many 11's in 99 =
3. 11 plus 13 =
4. 11 and 11 =
5. 5 lots of 11 =
6. 21 add 11 =
7. 48 take away 11 =
8. 11 times 11 =
9. 11 and 11 and 11 =
10. 11 more than 4 =

More or less

Double these numbers

9 _____   11 _____   17 _____
22 _____   35 _____   49 _____

Halve these numbers

24 _____   36 _____   50 _____
48 _____   94 _____   16 _____

53

12 times table

Trace over the number in the box

1 x 12 =	12	12 ÷ 12 = 1
2 x 12 =	24	24 ÷ 12 = 2
3 x 12 =	36	36 ÷ 12 = 3
4 x 12 =	48	48 ÷ 12 = 4
5 x 12 =	60	60 ÷ 12 = 5
6 x 12 =	72	72 ÷ 12 = 6
7 x 12 =	84	84 ÷ 12 = 7
8 x 12 =	96	96 ÷ 12 = 8
9 x 12 =	108	108 ÷ 12 = 9
10 x 12 =	120	120 ÷ 12 = 10
11 x 12 =	132	132 ÷ 12 = 11
12 x 12 =	144	144 ÷ 12 = 12

Multiplication grid by 12

X	1	2	3	4	5	6	7	8	9	10	11	12
12						72						144

Colour the squares below that are multiples of 12

111	112	113	114	115	116	117	118	119	120
121	122	123	124	125	126	127	128	129	130
131	132	133	134	135	136	137	138	139	140
141	142	143	144	145	146	147	148	149	150
151	152	153	154	155	156	157	158	159	160

Which number comes next?

1. 14 26 ☐ 50 ☐
2. 120 108 ☐ 84 ☐
3. 49 37 ☐ 13 ☐
4. 132 144 ☐ 168 ☐
5. 9 ☐ 33 45 ☐

Number facts

6 x 12 = ___   12 x 6 = ___
120 − 12 = ___   120 − 108 = ___
96 ÷ 12 = ___   96 ÷ 8 = ___
12 x 3 = ___   3 x 12 = ___
12 + 17 = ___   17 + 12 = ___

Time challenge

Start ___ Finish ___ Time taken ___   Start ___ Finish ___ Time taken ___

1. 2 x 12 = ___   11. 12 x 12 = ___
2. 25 + 12 = ___   12. 8 x 12 = ___
3. 132 ÷ 12 = ___   13. 6 x 12 = ___
4. 63 − 12 = ___   14. 9 x 12 = ___
5. 12 + 79 = ___   15. 5 x 12 = ___
6. 12 x 4 = ___   16. 3 x 12 = ___
7. 73 − 12 = ___   17. 11 x 12 = ___
8. 60 ÷ 12 = ___   18. 7 x 12 = ___
9. 43 + 12 = ___   19. 4 x 12 = ___
10. 12 x 9 = ___   20. 10 x 12 = ___

Maths words

1. 12 more than 6 = ___
2. 12 and 12 and 12 = ___
3. 3 lots of 12 = ___
4. 32 add 12 = ___
5. how many 12's in 96? = ___
6. 12 times 7 = ___
7. 12 and 13 = ___
8. 11 times 12 = ___
9. 94 take away 12 = ___
10. 42 minus 12 = ___

How many?
Fill in the addition wheel

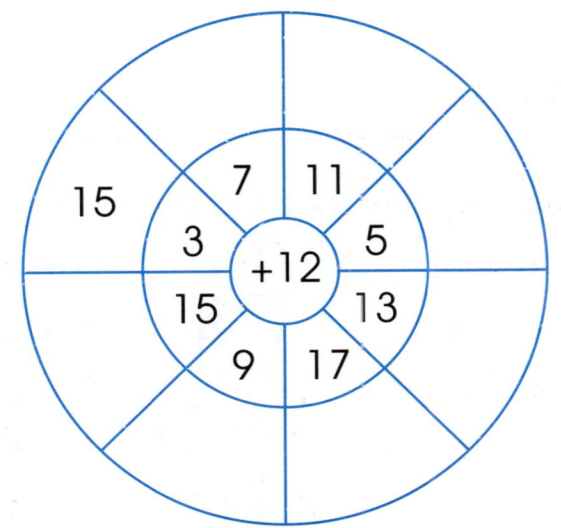

+ Addition (plus, adding on)

1.  + ___ = [   ]

___ + ___ = ___

2. 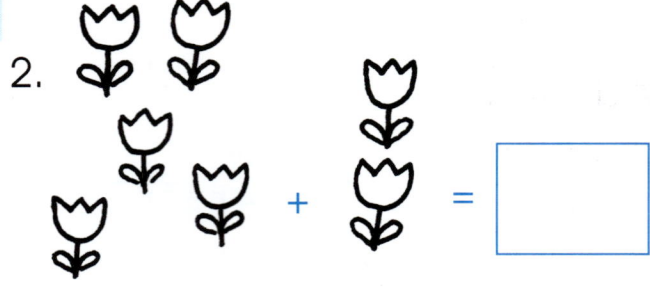 + ___ = [   ]

___ + ___ = ___

3. We had 4 lollies and we got 5 more.
How many lollies did we have altogether?

___ + ___ = ___

4. 7 boys and 6 girls were in the yard.
How many children were in the yard?

___ + ___ = ___

Draw pictures for these number sentences.

5.

4 + 2 = ___

6.

5 + 3 = ___

7. Add these as quickly as you can.

5 + 4 = ___  9 + 3 = ___  6 + 3 = ___

6 + 6 = ___ 4 + 8 = ___ 9 + 2 = ___

2 + 7 = ___ 7 + 5 = ___ 4 + 4 = ___

4 + 2 = ___ 5 + 5 = ___ 6 + 5 = ___

2 + 2 = ___ 3 + 7 = ___ 8 + 2 = ___

Vertical addition

Add these numbers using Tens and Units

T	U
1	2
+	5

T	U
	9
+	4

T	U
	7
+	6

T	U
	8
+	8

Now add using exchange with 10's

T	U
1	6
+ 1	7

T	U
2	3
+ 1	9

T	U
2	7
+ 4	5

T	U
5	5
+ 1	9

Addition grid

+	2	6	4	9	5	3	7	12	10	8	11	20
3												
9												
12												
2												
10												
5												

Addition wheels

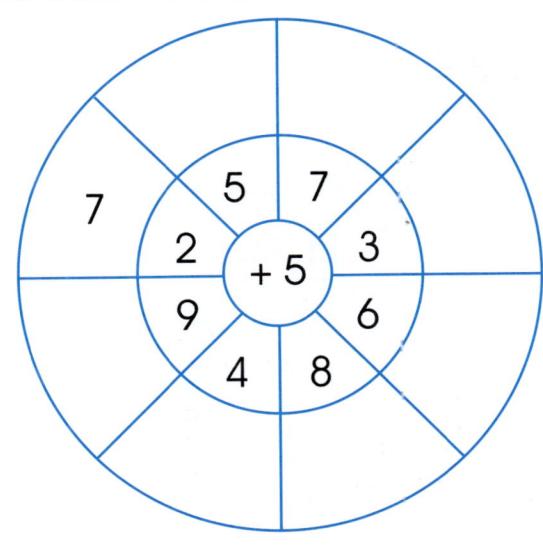

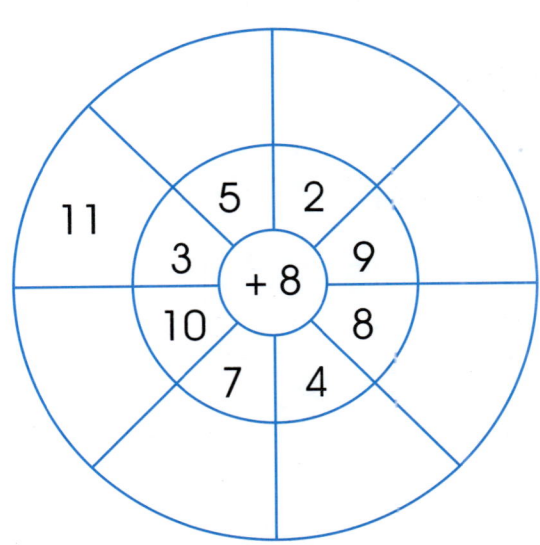

– Subtraction (take away, minus)

1.  5 - 2 = ☐

I had five apples, two were eaten. How many were left?

2. 6 - 2 = ☐

I had six flowers, two died. How many were left? _____

Now try these:

3. I had twelve eggs, I broke four. ____ – ____ = ☐
   How many were left? _____

4. There were five puppies, three ran away. ____ – ____ = ☐
   How many were left? _____

5. Tom had six toy cars, he lost one. ____ – ____ = ☐
   How many were left? _____

6. There were nine skittles, I knocked down four. ____ – ____ = ☐
   How many were left? _____

Subtraction wheels

Wheel 1: 15 – with numbers 14, 11, 7, 1, 5, 9, 2, 6, 8

Wheel 2: 20 – with numbers 16, 5, 11, 7, 13, 6, 19, 2

Do these as quickly as you can.

10 - 5 = ☐   3 - 2 = ☐   7 - 3 = ☐   6 - 2 = ☐

5 - 4 = ☐   9 - 2 = ☐   2 - 0 = ☐   8 - 3 = ☐

Vertical subtraction

T	U
1	4
−	3

T	U
	8
−	4

T	U
	9
−	2

T	U
	6
−	5

Now subtract, using exchange with 10's
Borrow 10 from Tens and add to Units

T	U
1	3
−	7

T	U
$\not{1}$	¹3
−	7
	6

subtract
—
take away

T	U
1	2
−	6

T	U
1	4
−	8

T	U
2	2
−	9

T	U
2	1
−	7

Subtraction grid

−	8	6	4	9	5	11	7	12	10
3									
4									
2									
0									

x Multiplication (groups of, times)

Sometimes when things are in groups it is easier to count them by multiplying. If you had 8 pairs of socks, it would be quicker to count by 2's.

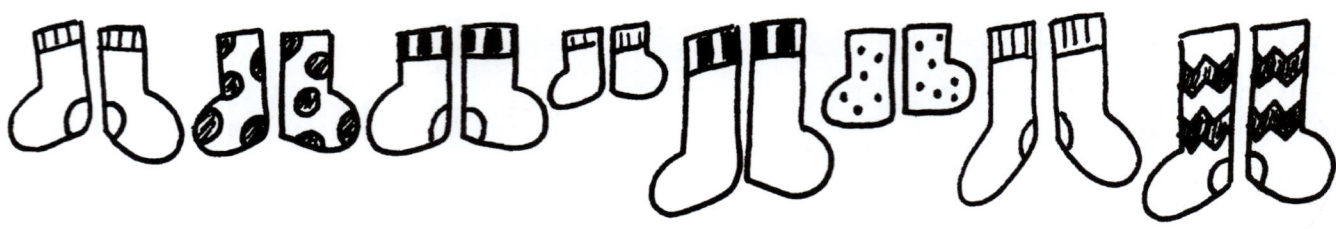

8 groups of 2 = 16.   8 x 2 = 16.

You can draw pictures, use symbols or learn times tables to help you count large numbers.

7 groups of 3
7 x 3 = 21

Now try these. You can use symbols to help you.

5 x 4 =

3 x 6 =

8 x 5 =

7 x 5 =

10 x 1 =

1 x 9 =

4 x 2 =

2 x 3 =

3 x 3 =

6 x 2 =

4 x 6 =

Sometimes we have a large group of things which we want to share out. This is called dividing.

12 marbles to be divided into 3 groups.

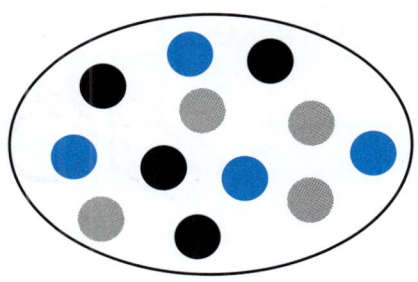  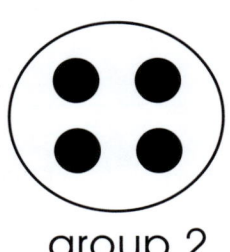 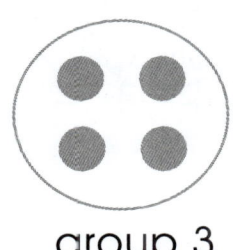

group 1   group 2   group 3

You can draw pictures, use symbols or learn times tables to help you divide large numbers.

$20 \div 5 =$ _____

$9 \div 3 =$ _____

$16 \div 4 =$ _____

$14 \div 7 =$ _____

$10 \div 2 =$ _____

$20 \div 10 =$ _____

$18 \div 3 =$ _____

$18 \div 2 =$ _____

$6 \div 3 =$ _____

$8 \div 4 =$ _____

So far we have looked at the times tables, addition, subtraction and division. Now all we need is lots of practice.

Time yourself using a stop watch.

Watch the sign so you aren't tricked.

Start _____ Finish _____ Time taken _____

5 + 4 = ____	7 + 5 = ____	6 ÷ 3 = ____
7 + 2 = ____	4 + 9 = ____	19 − 7 = ____
11 − 3 = ____	12 − 8 = ____	10 x 6 = ____
9 − 6 = ____	16 − 7 = ____	6 + 6 = ____
2 x 5 = ____	2 x 8 = ____	14 − 7 = ____
1 x 3 = ____	3 x 6 = ____	20 − 12 = ____
16 ÷ 4 = ____	12 ÷ 3 = ____	15 + 1 = ____
15 ÷ 3 = ____	20 ÷ 4 = ____	14 ÷ 2 = ____
3 + 7 = ____	1 + 9 = ____	7 + 6 = ____
8 − 4 = ____	11 − 2 = ____	10 x 2 = ____
2 x 4 = ____	5 x 5 = ____	22 + 6 = ____
10 ÷ 2 = ____	30 ÷ 6 = ____	13 − 6 = ____
4 x 8 = ____	9 x 4 = ____	24 ÷ 4 = ____
3 x 3 = ____	4 x 4 = ____	9 + 9 = ____
9 + 5 = ____	6 + 11 = ____	4 x 5 = ____
16 + 4 = ____	5 x 6 = ____	16 − 8 = ____
11 x 2 = ____	17 − 5 = ____	70 ÷ 10 = ____
21 − 13 = ____	3 x 10 = ____	2 x 8 = ____
14 + 5 = ____	20 ÷ 2 = ____	10 − 8 = ____
16 ÷ 4 = ____	3 + 13 = ____	15 + 7 = ____

Mix it up.

When you have had a lot of practice you should be ready for any number work.

Try some of these different ways of using numbers.

15 − ☐ = 5

4 x 10 + 5 = ☐

28 ÷ ☐ = 7

6 + ☐ + 6 = 19

☐ − 4 = 8

50 ÷ 10 = ☐

3 x ☐ = 15

3 + 4 + ☐ = 11

☐ ÷ 3 = 6

14 − 4 = ☐

9 x ☐ = 18

16 ÷ 4 = ☐

9 x ☐ = 27

17 − ☐ = 9

18 ÷ ☐ = 3

12 − 9 = ☐

5 + ☐ = 17

12 − 9 = ☐

5 + 9 = ☐

10 ÷ 10 = ☐

10 + ☐ = 30

☐ + 11 = 13

18 − ☐ = 13

9 ÷ ☐ = 9

☐ − 15 = 5

14 ÷ 2 = ☐

7 − ☐ = 7

6 + ☐ + 10 = 21

☐ x 3 = 15

20 − 11 = ☐

☐ ÷ 6 = 10

12 − 9 = ☐

6 + ☐ = 18

ANSWER PAGE

Page 34:
Multiplication grid by 2
4, 6, 8, 10, 12, 14, 16, 18, 20, 22, 24

Page 35:
Which number comes next?
1) 6, 12
2) 16, 12
3) 42, 46
4) 5, 7, 11
5) 47, 51

Number facts
7, 2, 14, 2, 11, 19, 7, 5, 14, 12, 11, 2

Time challenge		Maths words
1) 7	11) 10	1) 7
2) 11	12) 6	2) 14
3) 18	13) 14	3) 3
4) 12	14) 20	4) 12
5) 44	15) 8	5) 12
6) 12	16) 18	6) 16
7) 15	17) 12	7) 13
8) 22	18) 16	8) 10
9) 4	19) 4	9) 6
10) 15	20) 22	10) 25

How many?
12

Page 36:
Multiplication grid by 3
3, 6, 9, 12, 15, 21, 24, 27, 30, 33, 36

Page 37:
Which number comes next?
1) 6, 12
2) 36, 39, 42
3) 18, 15
4) 8, 14
5) 36, 30

Number facts
9, 12, 14, 12, 18, 9, 3, 14, 12, 3

Time challenge		Maths words
1) 11	11) 9	1) 3
2) 9	12) 33	2) 16
3) 13	13) 6	3) 9
4) 6	14) 18	4) 12
5) 6	15) 12	5) 5
6) 17	16) 24	6) 12
7) 8	17) 36	7) 9
8) 4	18) 15	8) 21
9) 5	19) 30	9) 34
10) 15	20) 21	10) 11

How many?
9, 3

Page 38:
Multiplication grid by 4
4, 8, 12, 20, 24, 28, 32, 40, 44, 48

Page 39:
Which number comes next?
1) 16, 24
2) 40, 36,
3) 45, 49
4) 54, 46
5) 9, 17

Number facts
10, 20, 13, 13, 12, 10, 20, 4, 13, 12

Time challenge		Maths words
1) 2	11) 12	1) 12
2) 3	12) 24	2) 12
3) 8	13) 28	3) 24
4) 17	14) 16	4) 11
5) 10	15) 8	5) 4
6) 14	16) 32	6) 17
7) 28	17) 36	7) 20
8) 5	18) 40	8) 21
9) 23	19) 44	9) 21
10) 13	20) 20	10) 33

How many Tens and Units?
1) 4 tens, 5 units. 2) 3 tens, 9 units.
3) 1 tens, 2 units. 4) 10 tens, 0 units.
5) 0 tens, 3 units.

Page 40:
Multiplication grid by 5
5, 10, 15, 20, 35, 40, 45, 55, 60

Page 41:
Which number comes next?
1) 20
2) 55, 50
3) 12, 22
4) 43, 33
5) 40, 50, 55

Number facts
15, 30, 13, 18, 45, 15, 30, 5, 18, 45

Time challenge		Maths words
1) 5	11) 20	1) 15
2) 15	12) 40	2) 9
3) 10	13) 25	3) 23
4) 12	14) 35	4) 15
5) 29	15) 55	5) 30
6) 8	16) 15	6) 12
7) 45	17) 45	7) 14
8) 36	18) 30	8) 39
9) 21	19) 60	9) 9
10) 60	20) 10	10) 10

Watch the sign
16, 15, 17, 24, 50, 15, 5, 5, 0

Page 42:
Multiplication grid by 6
12, 18, 30, 36, 42, 48, 54, 66, 72

Page 43:
Which number comes next?
1) 30, 42
2) 48, 36
3) 16, 28
4) 25, 13
5) 78, 90

Number facts
12, 21, 15, 48, 30, 12, 21, 6, 48, 30

Time challenge		Maths words
1) 11	11) 24	1) 12
2) 38	12) 42	2) 19
3) 42	13) 72	3) 30
4) 9	14) 54	4) 21
5) 5	15) 12	5) 13
6) 20	16) 48	6) 27
7) 66	17) 30	7) 48
8) 13	18) 66	8) 18
9) 26	19) 18	9) 17
10) 30	20) 36	10) 38

How many?
1) 60, 2) 7, 3) 24, 4) 12, 5) 3

Page 44:
Multiplication grid by 7
7, 21, 28, 35, 42, 49, 63, 70, 77, 84

Page 45:
Which number comes next?
1) 14, 28,
2) 35, 21
3) 30, 44
4) 69, 55
5) 39, 60

Number facts
9, 42, 22, 16, 2, 7, 42, 22, 7, 7

Time challenge		Maths words
1) 22	11) 42	1) 26
2) 12	12) 28	2) 21
3) 26	13) 63	3) 21
4) 63	14) 21	4) 21
5) 30	15) 56	5) 15
6) 8	16) 77	6) 20
7) 84	17) 70	7) 48
8) 49	18) 35	8) 63
9) 21	19) 49	9) 7
10) 55	20) 14	10) 3

Colour the shapes which show halves

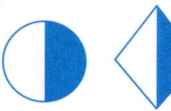  

Page 46:
Multiplication grid by 8
8, 16, 24, 32, 40, 48, 64, 72, 88, 96

Page 47:
Which number comes next?
1) 80, 96   2) 23, 7
3) 31, 47   4) 24, 16
5) 10, 26

Number facts
15, 4, 24, 13, 24, 15, 8, 24, 8, 24

Time challenge		Maths words		Tuck shop specials
1) 4	11) 24	1) 21		50c
2) 11	12) 56	2) 32		30c
3) 31	13) 80	3) 27		50c
4) 56	14) 32	4) 96		$1.20
5) 53	15) 64	5) 26		60c
6) 12	16) 96	6) 53		
7) 61	17) 48	7) 4		
8) 16	18) 72	8) 40		
9) 6	19) 16	9) 28		
10) 96	20) 40	10) 24		

ANSWER PAGE

Page 48:
Multiplication grid by 9
9, 18, 27, 54, 63, 72, 81, 90, 99, 108

Page 49:
Which number comes next?
1) 108, 126
2) 72, 54
3) 17, 35
4) 35, 17
5) 10, 37

Number facts
8, 36, 24, 26, 72, 9, 36, 9, 26, 72

Time challenge		Maths words
1) 81	11) 45	1) 27
2) 23	12) 72	2) 32
3) 12	13)108	3) 24
4) 25	14) 90	4) 6
5) 8	15) 27	5) 4
6) 27	16) 54	6) 23
7) 6	17) 81	7) 72
8) 28	18) 99	8) 28
9) 27	19) 63	9) 54
10) 45	20) 36	10) 33

Watch the sign
12, 8, 5, 26, 63

Page 50:
Multiplication grid by 10
10, 20, 40, 50, 60, 70, 80, 100, 110, 120

Page 51:
Which number comes next?
1) 30, 50
2) 80, 60
3) 77, 47
4) 33, 53
5) 32, 52

Number facts
50, 6, 31, 80, 75, 50, 10, 10, 80, 75

Time challenge		Maths words
1) 80	11) 70	01) 07
2) 43	12) 40	02) 19
3) 11	13)120	03) 60
4) 29	14) 90	04) 34
5) 59	15) 50	05) 80
6)100	16) 80	06) 23
7) 1	17) 30	07) 30
8)110	18)110	08) 47
9) 33	19) 60	09) 52
10)110	20) 20	10) 09

More or less
1) 11, 2) 7, 3) 12, 4) 4, 5) 17, 5) 1

Page 52:
Multiplication grid by 11
11, 22, 44, 55, 66, 88, 99, 110, 132

Page 53:
Which number comes next?
1) 34, 56
2) 110
3) 26, 48
4) 70, 48
5) 68, 90

Number facts
99, 12, 45, 66, 34, 99, 11, 11, 66, 34

Time challenge		Maths words
1) 99	11) 22	1) 54
2) 12	12) 66	2) 9
3) 27	13) 99	3) 24
4) 46	14) 33	4) 22
5)121	15) 77	5) 55
6) 7	16)110	6) 32
7) 83	17) 44	7) 37
8) 29	18) 88	8)121
9) 52	19)132	9) 33
10) 1	20) 55	10) 15

More of less
Double these numbers
18, 22, 34, 44, 70, 98

Halve these numbers
12, 18, 25, 24, 47, 8

Page 54:
Multiplication grid by 10
12, 24, 36, 40, 60, 84, 96, 108, 120, 132

Page 55:
Which number comes next?
1) 38, 62
2) 96, 72
3) 25, 1
4) 156, 180
5) 21, 57

Number facts
72, 108, 8, 36, 29, 72, 12, 12, 36, 29

Time challenge		Maths words
1) 24	11)144	01) 18
2) 37	12) 96	02) 36
3) 11	13) 72	03) 36
4) 51	14)108	04) 44
5) 91	15) 60	05) 08
6) 48	16) 36	06) 84
7) 61	17) 132	07) 25
8) 5	18) 84	08)132
9) 55	19) 48	09) 82
10)108	20)120	10) 30

How many? Fill in the addition wheel

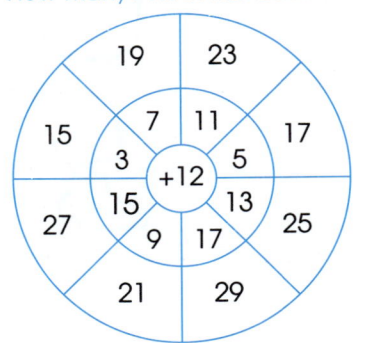

Page 56:
+ addition (plus, adding on)
1) 3 + 2 = 5   2) 5 + 2 = 7
3) 4 + 5 = 9   4) 7 + 6 = 13
5) 4 + 2 = 6   6) 5 + 3 = 8
7) 9   12   9
   12   12   11
   9   12   8
   6   10   11
   4   10   10

Page 57:
Vertical addition
17, 13, 13, 16
33, 42, 72, 74

Addition grid

+	2	6	4	9	5	3	7	12	10	8	11	20
3	5	9	7	12	8	6	10	15	13	11	14	23
9	11	15	13	18	14	12	16	21	19	17	20	29
12	14	18	16	21	17	15	19	24	22	20	23	32
2	4	8	6	11	7	5	9	14	12	10	13	22
10	12	16	14	19	15	13	17	22	20	18	21	30
5	7	11	9	14	10	8	12	17	15	13	16	25

Addition wheels

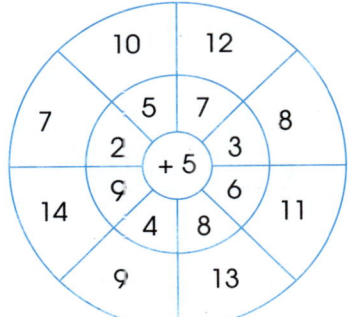

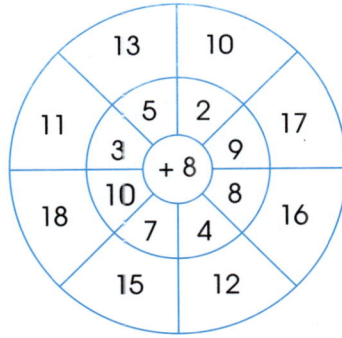

ANSWER PAGE

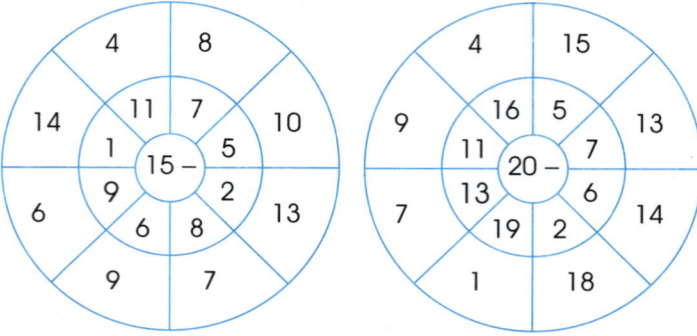

Page 58:
– subtraction (take away, minus)
1) 3, 2) 4
3) 12 – 4 = 8, 4) 5 – 3 = 2
5) 6 – 1 = 5,   6) 9 – 4 = 5

Subtraction wheels

Page 59:
5, 1, 4, 4,
1, 7, 2, 5

Vertical subtraction
11, 4, 7, 1

Subtract, using exchange with 10's
6, 6, 6, 13, 14

Subtraction grid

–	8	6	4	9	5	11	7	12	10
3	5	3	1	6	2	8	4	9	7
4	4	2	0	5	1	7	3	8	6
2	6	4	2	7	3	9	5	10	8
0	8	6	4	9	5	11	7	12	10

Page 60:
x Multiplication (groups of, times)
20, 18, 40, 35, 10, 9, 8, 6, 9, 12, 24

Page 61:
÷ Division (dividing, sharing)
4, 3, 4, 2, 5, 2, 6, 9, 2, 2

Page 62:

9	12	2
9	13	12
8	4	60
3	9	12
10	16	7
3	18	8
4	4	16
5	5	7
10	10	13
4	9	20
8	25	28
5	5	7
32	36	6
9	16	18
14	17	20
20	30	8
22	12	7
8	30	16
19	10	2
4	16	22

Page 63:

10	3
45	14
4	1
7	20
12	2
5	5
5	1
4	20
18	7
10	0
2	5
4	5
3	9
8	60
6	3
3	12
12	

Grammar

What is Grammar?

Grammar is about knowing how to put words together in the correct order to make sense. Each word in a sentence has its purpose and when you know that purpose and follow the rules you will be writing and speaking meaningful sentences.

The word groups we will be looking at in this book are:

Nouns   **Prepositions**

Pronouns   **Articles**

Adjectives   **Conjunctions**

Verbs   **Interjections**

Adverbs

Additionally we will have a look at tense, and briefly discuss punctuation.
What is punctuation?. Full stops. Question marks. Commas.
Along the way you will find a number of self-testing exercises which should prove both helpful and entertaining.

From Professor Mentor's list, find the hidden words.

```
o t v w n a d v e r b s u
p r e p o s i t i o n s o
d k r i u k l b n p p i k
e p b t n d l l k r w t a
b m s e s f e n r o f e r
o l a d g e w e g n a n t
c o n j u n c t i o n s i
n l t g m e s n r u t g c
o e b r o w n b o n b r l
a d j e c t i v e s g r e
i n t e r j e c t i o n s
```

Grammar is not difficult it is just a matter of finding the correct words and placing them in the correct order.

Nouns

What are Nouns?

Nouns are names of people, places, animals or things.
The name we give to anything we may see, hear, touch, taste, smell or imagine is a noun.

Name of Person Place or Thing

There are four kinds of nouns.

Common nouns - These apply to any one of a type of person, place, animal or thing: apple, computer, pen, lake, book, dog, chair.

Use the correct list words in the sentence below:

Patch is my pet _____.

I work on the _____ in class at school.

An _____ a day, keeps the doctor away.

"Which _____ are you reading?"

Can you think of more?

_____

_____

Proper nouns - These apply to names of a particular person, place, animal or thing and is usually written with a capital letter: Sharon, London, July, Monday, Christmas, Mexico, Uncle John, Main Street.

Use the correct list words in the sentence below:

At _____ we put presents under the tree.

August is the month after _____.

Aunty Mary and _____ came for dinner.

_____ is the capital city of England.

Can you think of more?

_____

_____

Collective Nouns
- These apply to a group of people, places, animals or things: swarm, class, herd, collection, group.

Use the correct list words in the sentences below:

A _____ of bees went into the hive.

I saw a _____ of cattle in the field.

Mrs Green taught the year two _____.

Tom had a large _____ of marbles.

Can you think of more?

_____

_____

Abstract nouns
- These apply to those things that cannot be touched but can be thought about: courage, happiness, sleep, freedom, ideas, dreams, beauty, pain, safety, wisdom, danger.

Use the correct list words in the sentences below:

When we _____ we have _____.

He had a _____ in his knee.

He showed great _____ when he rescued the cat.

Can you think of more?

_____

_____

_____

Nouns can be the name of one thing (singular) boat, ruler, car, spoon, book, woman or the name of more than one thing (plural) boats, rulers, cars, spoons, books, women.

Can you think of more?

Singular   Plural

Butterfly

Butterflies

Pronouns

What are pronouns?

Pronouns are the words we use instead of nouns. Examples: I, mine, me, she, they, their, them, you, your. All these words are used instead of the actual names of people or animals.

Rewrite these sentences using a pronoun in place of the underlined word.
<u>Susie</u> went to the shop.

_____

Sam saw <u>Ann</u>, <u>Janet</u> <u>and</u> <u>John</u> near the fence.

_____

"Did <u>Kate</u> <u>and</u> <u>Bill</u> come with you?"

_____

Can you think of more?

_____

The examples above are **personal pronouns**.

Demonstrative pronouns are: this, that, these, those.

Interrogative pronouns are those words that ask a question: who, what, whose, which, whoever, whatever, when.

Indefinite pronouns are used to refer to persons or things without being specific: nobody, some, either, few, everything, none, other.

Read the sentence and write which type of pronoun is underlined.

"<u>Why</u> are you so happy?" _____.

We choose <u>those</u> pizzas for lunch, too. _____.

Jack put <u>everything</u> he needed in the bag. _____.

Write these sentences using one of each type of pronoun.

_____

_____

_____

'Michael and I are going to the circus. It will be great!'
In this example 'I' is a pronoun, and so is 'It'.

We may use pronouns to stand in place of the names of people or things.

Try to include pronouns in the following:

_____ is eating birthday cake.

Bill and _____ went to the house.

_____ sock has a hole in _____ .

Can you see _____ ?

_____ looks like _____ might rain.

A few boys are riding _____ bicycles.

Where is _____ hat?

Do _____ feel better now?

pronouns

Draws circles around the pronouns in the following sentences:

Please take me to the zoo.

I have not been for ages.

It is one of my favourite places.

John and his mother went last Saturday and they had the best time.

Write your own sentences using pronouns:

_____

_____

_____

_____

Personal pronouns

first person: I, me, myself, mine

second person: you, your

third person: he, she, it, they, them

My cat

Your cat

Her cat

Adjectives

What are adjectives?

Adjectives are words that describe or give information about a noun or pronoun. They tell us about the size, number, colour and quality of a noun or pronoun.

For example:
It was a dark and stormy night.
            adjective   adjective   noun

or
The small boy has long hair.
   adjective noun   adjective noun

Would you like to try?

The _____ grass needs watering.
She is a _____ girl.
They went to the shop to buy _____ fruit.
The _____ snake shifted along the ground.

In the above examples each of the adjectives come before the noun, but not all adjectives are placed this way:

The dog is old and tired.
  noun   adjective   adjective

Toys are <u>fun</u>
Winter is <u>cold</u> and <u>windy</u>.

Match the adjective to the noun:

adjective	noun
clever	ride
fast	night
dark	child
tall	building
red	frog
green	door
open	noise
loud	face

Sometimes a number of adjectives are used to better describe a noun. Such as:

The big, brown, lazy dog
adjective adjective adjective noun

or

The house is old, dark, smelly and spooky.
noun   adjective adjective adjective   adjective

Would you like to try?

The _____ _____ rain fell all day.
I see a _____ _____ _____ shadow.
Frogs are often _____ and _____.
The _____ _____ car went down the street.

Adjectives may take three forms

adjective	comparative adjective	superlative adjective
many	more	most
long	longer	longest
high	higher	highest
bad	worse	worst
short	shorter	shortest
good	better	best

Now you try

low	_____	_____
_____	_____	smallest
_____	wider	_____

long

longer

longest

Write your own sentences using the following adjectives:

happy, bright, black, rude, big.

_____

_____

_____

_____

Verbs

What are verbs?

Verbs are 'doing' words. They tell us what a person, animal or thing is doing. Without verbs to explain what is happening, sentences would make no sense at all.

Without a verb the sentence
"The dog barked at Tom." Would be
"The dog at Tom". That doesn't make sense!

Run, jump, play, eat, know, wear and laugh are all verbs.
They describe the action of the sentence.

Try inserting the following verbs into the sentences:

blows, dug, flown, jumped, ran, run, sang, speed, went

John has _____ in an aeroplane.

The wind _____ very hard.

_____ for your life.

Sarah _____ to school today.

They _____ to the train station.

The racing cars _____ around the track.

Her horse _____ the fence.

At school we _____ a new song.

The men _____ a large hole.

Circle the verbs in the following sentences.

Ducks are swimming in the pond.
I am going to sleep now.
Have you been thinking about me?
I love you very much.
Are you staying home today?

Verbs may change form depending on a number of factors.
See how a change of personal pronoun alters the
singular and plural of 'to run'.

personal pronoun	*singular*	*plural*
first person	run	we run
second person	you run	you run
third person	he/she/it runs	they run

Circle the doing words

p	r	e	s	o	s	i	t	i	o	n	s
j	u	m	p	e	d	f	b	a	k	e	d
e	n	b	e	n	d	l	l	s	r	w	t
b	m	s	e	s	f	o	n	a	o	f	k
o	l	a	d	g	e	w	e	n	t	a	i
r	o	n	w	u	n	n	t	g	o	n	s
a	l	t	a	m	b	u	r	n	t	t	s
n	e	b	l	o	w	s	b	o	n	b	e
a	d	j	k	c	t	i	v	d	u	g	d
i	s	t	e	c	o	n	t	a	c	t	n

run
blows
dug
flown
jumped
ran
sang
speed
went
walk
baked
kissed
burnt

Some verbs change when we speak about different times:

past	I stayed at home yesterday.
present	I am staying at home today.
future	I will stay at home tomorrow.

Write sentences using the following verbs:

walk, baked, singing, burnt, kissed, contact

Adverbs

What are adverbs?

Adverbs add meaning to a verb. They tell us more about the verb. Many adverbs are actually adjectives with ly on the end, as:

adjective	adverb	adjective	adverb
slow	slowly	hungry	hungrily
quick	quickly	fair	fairly
busy	busily	deep	deeply
loud	loudly	high	highly
sweet	sweetly	hard	hardly
secret	secretly	just	justly
happy	happily	bare	barely

Beware. Not all words ending with ly are adverbs. consider: friendly, kindly, sly, silly. Other words ending with ly can be either adverbs or adjectives, depending on how they are used: only and early.

Write sentences using only or early as an adverb and an adjective.

_____

_____

_____

_____

_____

Adverbs ending with ly tend to describe manner, emphasis, degree, frequency, duration and probability as:

manner	emphasis	degree
happily	certainly	strongly
highly	positively	totally

frequency	duration	probability
rarely	briefly	probably
normally	permanently	definitely

Adverbs also determine time and place:
now, later, soon, tomorrow, outside, somewhere, here, there

Choose the correct adverb for each sentence.

I will come to your house _____ .
Doug ran _____ to ride on his bike.
_____ we are _____ .

Adverbs may also ask questions:
'How are you going?'
'When will you be back?'
'Where did you put the ball?'
'Why did you run off when I called you?'

Draw circles around the adverbs in the following sentences:

The ducks are swimming smoothly on the pond.
Kathy easily opened the old door.
'Go away.' he said angrily.
She happily skipped all the way to school.

Write your own sentences using the following adverbs:

strongly, gently, badly, soon, when.

Conjunctions

What are conjunctions?

Conjunctions are 'joining' words, that join together words or parts of a sentence.

Joining two words: knife and fork, poor but happy, rain or shine.

Some other words used as conjunctions are:
but, both, so, yet, as well as, therefore, nor, also.

Write your own sentences using conjunctions:

_____

_____

_____

_____

Interjections

What are interjections?

Interjections are small exclamation words which are used to express feelings. Sometimes they are actual words and sometimes merely sounds. oh, ah, hey, hi, yuk, ha, phew and gosh are all interjections.

Circle the interjections.

Wow! I really like that bike.　　　　　That was a near miss. Phew!

Write your own sentences using interjections:

_____

_____

_____

Prepositions

What are prepositions?

Prepositions show relationships between nouns and/or pronouns.

Prepositions are often very short words:
on, over, with, at, by, for, in.

At school, On your mark, In time, With fries, For Christmas.

Circle the prepositions in the following sentences:

Billy sat on the grass.
He jumped over the fence.
Kelly walked with her mother.
I will see you after lunch.

Write your own sentences and circle the prepositions in them:

What are prepositions?

Some prepositions consist of two or three words:
instead of, aside from, in consideration of.

Write your own sentences containing these prepositions:

Articles

What are articles?

Articles are small words placed in front of the noun.

Articles fall into two categories:

Definite articles.   Indefinite articles.

There are only three articles: **The**... definite article,
A... indefinite article, **An**... indefinite article.

When we use **the** we are speaking of a particular thing.

Link the correct sentence to the picture shown.
Colour the picture.

Roger is driving the car.

The bathroom tap is leaking.

A and **An** are used when we are speaking
of a general something.

I saw a duck today.

There is a new girl at school.

An apple a day keeps the doctor away.

A is generally used before a word starting with a consonant: (see page 17)

a ship	a key	a cup
a rabbit	a wheel	a bucket

An is generally used before a word starting with a vowel:

an aeroplane	an Inuit	an iceberg
an orange	an umbrella	an invention

Gender

What is gender?

Gender refers to the sex of a person or animal.

Masculine: boy, man, prince, father, uncle, son
Feminine: girl, woman, princess, mother, aunt, daughter.

Some nouns can refer to either a male or a female:
child, adult, parent, teacher, cousin

Can you think of others?

Capital letters

What are capital letters?

Capital letters are the large, or upper case, letters which appear at the start of a sentence.

Capital letters are used for the first letter of a sentence, the first letter of a name or proper noun, such as David, Sarah, London, Christmas.

Rewrite these sentences using capital letters.

dan and rebecca went on a holiday.

they sailed to hawaii on a cruise ship

Each lowercase letter has a capital form as well

lowercase: a b c d e f g h i j k l m n o p q r s t u v w x y z
capital: A B C D E F G H I J K L M N O P Q R S T U V W X Y Z

What are vowels and consonants?

Vowels are: a, e, i, o, u
These are letters which can be sounded alone.

Consonants are: b c d f g h j k l m n p q r s t v w x y z

are letters which can only be sounded with a vowel.

81

Tenses

Tense is used to indicate the time in which the 'doing' of a verb takes place.

There are three tenses we will consider here:

Past tense —   It has already happened.

Present tense —   It is happening now.

Future tense —   It has not yet happened.

Examples of words as they change tense:

Past	Present	Future
I had	I have	I will have
I did	I am doing	I will do
I rode	I am riding	I will ride
I read	I am reading	I will read
I cut	I am cutting	I will cut
I stood	I am standing	I will stand
I laid	I am laying	I will lay
I saw	I see	I will see

Would you like to try?

Past	Present	Future
I was		
	I win	
I bought		I will choose
	I am flying	
I crept		I will get
	I am keeping	

Which tense?

Circle the correct tense for the following:

1. Can you come to the movies on Saturday? Past Present Future

2. He was riding his bicycle. Past Present Future

3. Have you been on holiday in the past year? Past Present Future

4. I an going to learn to play the piano. Past Present Future

1. Present 2. Past 3. Past 3. Future

82

Write three sentences, each with a different tense:

_____

_____

Beware of jumping tenses

Always be consistent about the tense of the verb.
If you write about something in the past you should
keep in the past all the way through your piece of
writing. Don't mix the past with the present.

The two boys will run joyfully through the winding streets.
The air is fresh and they felt completely happy.

Rewrite the above two sentences so they show a consistent tense.

Personal pronouns quick quiz

Choose the word from each pair in brackets to make a correct sentence:

1. You look a lot like (he/him).

2. They all went except (we/us).

3. What would you girls do without (us/we) boys?

4. That's between you and (she/her)

1. him   2. us   3. us   4. her

He gave a present
to my brother and (me/I).

This is just between
you and (me/I).

I   me

Punctuation

What is punctuation?

Punctuation is designed to assist the reader interpret written words in a meaningful way.

We have previously discussed capital letters, now we shall look at other aspects of punctuation.

Full stops (sometimes referred to as periods)

act as stop signs at the end of a sentence, unless that sentence is a question or an exclamation. Without full stops sentences would run together and make no sense.

Add the full stops to these sentences.

Martin went walking by the river He saw Angela on the sand She called out to say hello

Question marks (sometimes referred to as the query) are used instead of full stops at the end of a sentence that asks a question.

What are you hiding?   Did you see that?   Who threw that stone?   Why?

Write a question of your own (don't forget the question mark).

Exclamation marks are included at the end of sentences where the writer needs to express anger, danger, humour, joy or fear, or to indicate someone is shouting.

Fantastic!   Stop!   Look out!

It's a boy!   Help!

84

Commas indicate a brief pause, or separate different sections of longer sentences.

The zoo held lions, tigers, penguins and birds of every kind.

Quotation marks (sometimes referred to as inverted commas) are used to show words that are directly spoken.

"Come for a ride with me," said Jennifer.
Simon said, "Sorry, I can't do it right now."
"There is," he said, "no way out of here."

Would you like to try?

From silly to sense
Circle the incorrect word in each sentence and write the word you think it should be.

There are lions on the birthday cake.

Aeroplanes fly high in the window.

May I space your new book?

John and Jenny took the stair into town.

I put worms on my breakfast toast.

I can hear the pencil ringing.

Exclamation marks are used after:
Something is shouted,
"Look out!"

A command is given,
"Do it now!"

A strong feeling is expressed,
"I feel sick!"

Verb forms

A verb used without any indication of person, number or tense is referred to as the infinitive form. This is the basic form of a verb. Often the infinitive form is proceeded by 'to,' as: to jump, to walk.

A verb which is formed by adding 'ed' or 'd' to the end is referred to as the past tense. as: jumped, walked.

Although there are other forms of verbs we will concern ourselves with only the above.

As:

Infinite form	Past tense
hope	hoped
boil	boiled
fill	filled
watch	watched
vanish	vanished

Would you like to try?

love

_____ backed

load

answer

Add ed or ing to these verbs. Watch out, if you have to double a consonant!

hop   hopped   hopping

wish

skip

Remember:

To change a verb into the past tense add **ed**. (jump/jumped - play/played).

If the word ends with an **e**, add **d**. (type/typed - like/liked).

If the verb ends in a **y**, change the **y** to **i** and add **ed**. (study/ studied - try/tried).

Try some of your own:

_____

_____

_____

Irregular verbs

There are verbs which do not conform to the usual verb pattern, these are called irregular verbs. In some, the infinite form and the past tense are the same, as:

Infinite form	Past tense
cut	cut
set	set
hurt	hurt
cost	cost

Can you think of others?

Infinite form	Past tense
_____	_____
_____	_____
_____	_____

Write sentences for 2 of these verbs.

_____

_____

speak

spoke

Some irregular verbs have different words for the infinite form and the past tense as:

begin	began
speak	spoke
think	thought
fight	fought
freeze	froze

Can you think of others?

Infinite form	Past tense
_____	_____
_____	_____

Write sentences for the past tense of. bring and know

_____

_____

To show the importance of correct punctuation, try reading the following section from Wind in the Willows, without, and then, with punctuation.

the gentlemen behind clapped their hands and applauded and toad heard them saying how well she does it fancy a washerwoman driving a car as well as that the first time toad went a little faster then faster still and faster he heard the gentlemen call out warningly be careful washerwoman

Now read it again, this time with the correct punctuation.

The gentlemen behind clapped their hands and applauded, and toad heard them saying, "How well she does it! Fancy a washerwoman driving a car as well as that, the first time!"
Toad went a little faster, then faster still, and faster. He heard the gentlemen call out warningly, "Be careful, washerwoman!"

Insert the correct punctuation in the following:

when it's summer in australia
what season is it in england

ouch that hurt

let's go now said penny

look ahead on the road

Re-write the sentence with correct punctuation and capitals.

Now try this one:

oh let me in let me in I am cold and I am so wet exclaimed a child that stood crying at the door and knocking for admittance while the rain poured down and the wind made all the windows rattle

Unscramble

Unscramble the lines of the following nursery rhymes and write them so they make sense:

This that jack built is the house.

_____

What made of are little girls?

_____

The clock up the mouse ran.

_____

Here around the mulberry bush we go.

_____

Over the woods and through the river.

_____

Old old soul Cole was a merry King.

_____

Polly on the kettle put.

_____

In a Little corner Jack Horner sat.

_____

Quite Mary contrary Mary.

_____

Sat Little on Muffet Miss tuffet a.

_____

Helpful hints

Nouns can sometimes be used as an adjective when they are combined with another noun:
apple pie, fire engine, chain letter, word pattern.
Adjectives do not change. They remain the same whether they refer to singular or plural, masculine or feminine. As: red rose/red roses, fast train/fast trains, tall men/tall women

The is the most frequently used word in the English language.

That/Which These two words often cause confusion. And are frequently used interchangeably.

> **That** should be used when referring to something specific, as: Did you see the sleek red car that sped down the street?

> **Which** is used when referring to a general, non-defined something: There are many red cars which speed down streets.

And there is nothing wrong with beginning a sentence with and, if doing so it assists the flow as: The ship endured the raging storm throughout that long, long night. And with morning came the calm.

Anyone/Any one
Anyone is used when referring to a single person in a general way as anyone could see it. Any one refers to a person more specifically, as any one could see it.

Adverbs
Remember the most common adverbs end in ly. (wisely, wearily).
If you have difficulty with spelling remember to check a dictionary.
Use short sentences where possible. long sentences often confuse the reader.

Gender nouns
Match these male and female nouns

groom	heroine
stallion	niece
monk	sister
brother	hen
hero	bride
uncle	nun
rooster	mare

Can you think of three more?

Nouns
Adverbs
Gender Nouns

Revision

Write your own sentences using a proper noun as well as an abstract one:

_____

_____

_____

Circle the nouns in the following:

Jack and Jill
went up the hill
to fetch a pail of water.
Jack fell down
and broke his crown
and Jill came tumbling after.

Up Jack got
and home did trot
as fast as he could caper.
He went to bed
to mend his head
with vinegar and brown paper.

Mary had a little lamb,
It's fleece was white as snow.
Everywhere that Mary went,
The lamb was sure to go.
It followed her to school one day,
Which was against the rules.
It made the children laugh and play,
To see a lamb at school.

Jack Jill hill pail water crown home bed head vinegar paper
Mary lamb fleece snow school day rules children

91

Once is enough

Many speakers and writers use expressions which combine two or more words that say the same thing.

Circle the words that could be left out of the following sets:

join together

both alike

new innovation

divide up

just recently

past history

sink down

small in size

absolute perfection

return back

cooperate together

few in number

may possibly

repeat again

unite together

grateful thanks

Can you think of others?

_____

_____

_____

Double negative

A double negative is when two negative words appear in the same sentence. The second negative cancels out the first, as: I can't do nothing. Although this is intended to mean the speaker can not do something, if one can't do nothing, then clearly they can do something.

Consider: I haven't got no time to play.

I can't hardly wait until my holidays.

He can't do nothing.

You haven't heard nothing yet.

Rewrite these sentences.

_____

_____

_____

_____

negative + negative = positive

Some words with similar spelling, and sounding alike, have completely different meanings. These are called homophones.

Consider the following:

boy	buoy	cheep	cheap
dear	deer	curb	kerb
desert	dessert	pain	pane
ore	oar	miner	minor
rap	wrap	carrot	carat
hole	whole	fore	four
loan	lone	pale	pail
right	write	sell	cell
no	know	ewe	you

Write sentences using 4 groups of homophones. 1 group is the 2 words which sound the same but have different spelling e.g. right, write.

_____

_____

_____

_____

Wordsearch using the above words.

```
T X D Z H L T Y T A F S B P Q X C U P E O A W K V
Y Y M Y L O S N C K O M F X N M U D D M X O O Q F
X S K E R M R S H F R Y D L I K S E D I A E O O T
O J C R Y P V Y E M E A E R E C E S I N N V F G N
G X A N F P A Y E T G C A T W A L E Z O D S W R Z
A C I P O E W I P V N U R P H R L R L R L V E C E
U H R X U N S B N Y O L W E O A P T L F U F Y D V
Z O S Y R X G O Z Y J H T N L T R D O I O Q G Y Y
X L O H V I P Y V K J I E N E W T Z S U I F I Z V
N E D E E R G A F M R G O A R I L E S W S R P A T
L S R T W Q M H N W Q V H R S V O N D H I A I Y I
A U L Z K E G I T E J Z B U O Y A Y E R R T M J Y
W C D W T E K M N P P R W N O Z N F S W U V P C V
C H F V Z A R D P E T A A X C U O Y S Y G W W U E
C Z K S D C K B Y A R P L L M V R C E T R H Y R B
J Q Y M N A K N O W I C C E Z D E F R I B R N B L
U G Z Q C H E A P S K L H H A F H E T R S O O V R
```

93

Let's have some fun

Compose your own stories by filling in the missing words. While covering the story below pencil in words of your choice.

A adjective _____
B noun _____
C noun _____
D adjective _____
E adjective _____
F living noun _____
G relative _____
H superlative adj. _____
I superlative adj. _____
J adjective _____
K colour _____
L article of dress _____
M article of dress _____
N relative _____
O adjective _____

Transfer the words you wrote above into the indicated excerpt from *Little Red Riding Hood*

A long time ago, in a _____ _____ at the
         <small>A</small>   <small>B</small>

edge of a _____ , there lived a _____ _____
         <small>C</small>   <small>D</small>   <small>E</small>

_____ and her _____ . This _____ _____ _____
<small>F</small>   <small>G</small>   <small>D</small>   <small>E</small>   <small>F</small>

was the _____ _____ _____ there ever was.
        <small>H</small>   <small>I</small>   <small>F</small>

She was always dressed in a _____ _____
                            <small>J</small>   <small>K</small>

_____ and _____ that her _____ had made for
<small>L</small>   <small>M</small>   <small>N</small>

her, so that everyone began calling her

_____ _____ _____ _____ .
<small>O</small>   <small>K</small>   <small>L</small>   <small>M</small>

94

More fun

Now you know how it works, have someone ask you for the required words and have them pencil these into the indicated spaces.

noun
adjective
verb
ncme

Excerpt from *The Stonecutter*

Once upon a time their lived a _____, who went
PROFESSION

every day to a _____ _____ in the side of a
ADJECTIVE   NOUN

_____ _____ and cut slabs for _____ or
ADJECTIVE   NOUN   PLURAL NOUN

for _____. He understood very well the kinds of
PLURAL NOUN

_____ wanted for the different purposes, and as
PLURAL NOUN

he was a _____ _____ he had _____
ADJECTIVE   NOUN   NUMBER

customers.

Excerpt from *The Emperor's new clothes*

Many, many years ago lived a _____, who
NOUN

thought so much of _____ _____ that he
ADJECTIVE   PLURAL NOUN

spent all his _____ in order to obtain them. His
NOUN

only ambition was to be always well _____. He
PAST TENSE VERB

did not care for his _____, and the _____ did
PLURAL NOUN   NOUN

not amuse him; the only thing, in fact, he thought

anything of was to _____ out and show a new
VERB

_____ of _____.
NOUN   PLURAL NOUN

95

Wordsearch
Answers

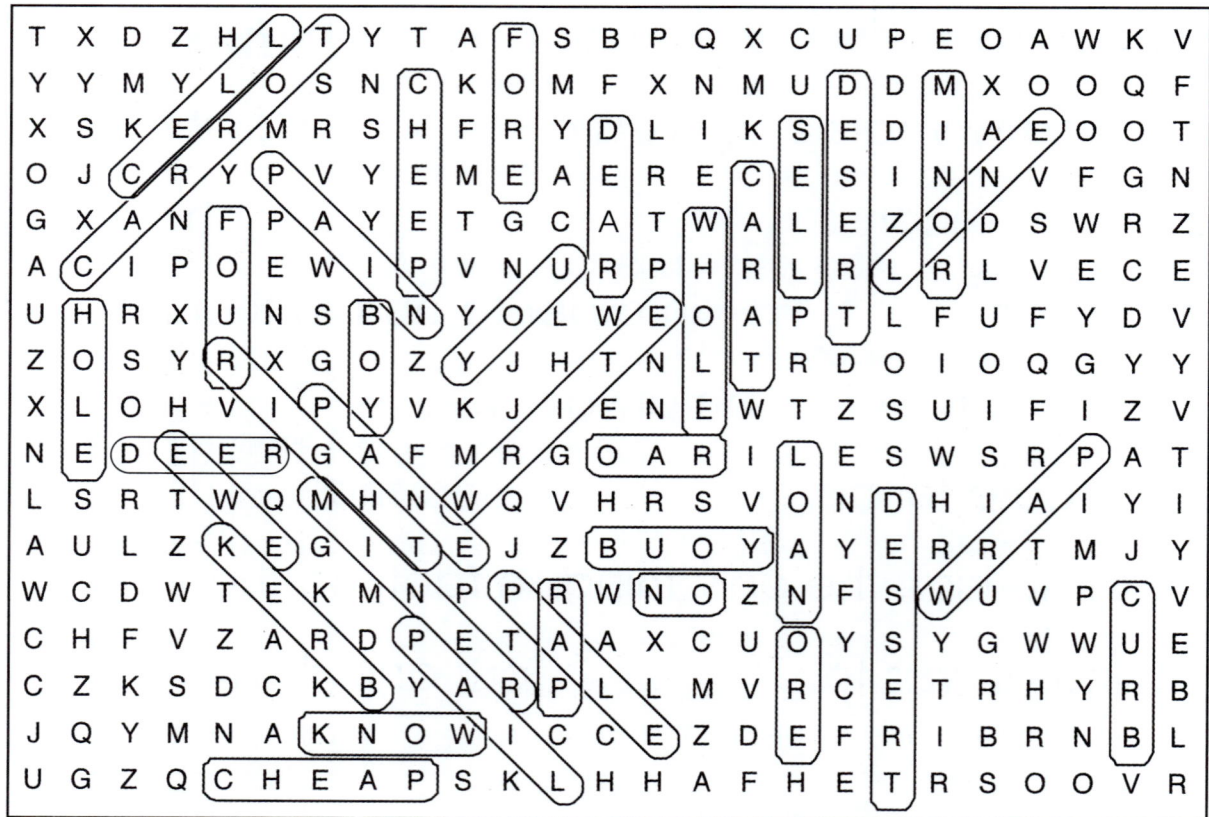

Page 67

```
o  t  v  w  n (a  d  v  e  r  b) s  u
p  r  e  p  o  s  i  t  i  o  n  s  o
d  k  r  i  u  k  l  b  n  p  p  i  k
e  p  b  t  n  d  l  l  k  r  w  t  a
b  m  s  e  s  f  e  n  r  o  e  n  r
o  l  a  d  g  e  w  e  g  n  a  n  t
c  o  n  j  u  n  c  t  i  o  n  s  i
n  l  t  g  m  e  s  n  r  u  t  g  c
o  e  b  r  o  w  n  b  o  n  b  r  l
a  d  j  e  c  t  i  v  e  s  g  r  e
i  n  t  e  r  j  e  c  t  i  o  n  s
```

Page 75

```
p  e  s  o  s  i  t  i  o  n  s
j  u  m  p  e  d  f  b  a  k  e  d
e  n  b  e  n  d  l  s  r  w  t
b  m  s  e  s  f  o  n  a  o  f  k
o  l  a  d  g  e  w  e  n  t  a  i
r  o  n  w  u  n  n  t  g  o  n  s
n  e  t  a  m  b  u  r  n  t  t  s
a  d  b  l  o  w  s  b  o  n  b  e
i  s  t  e  c  o  n  t  a  c  t  n
```

Page 93

Number
Problem
Solving

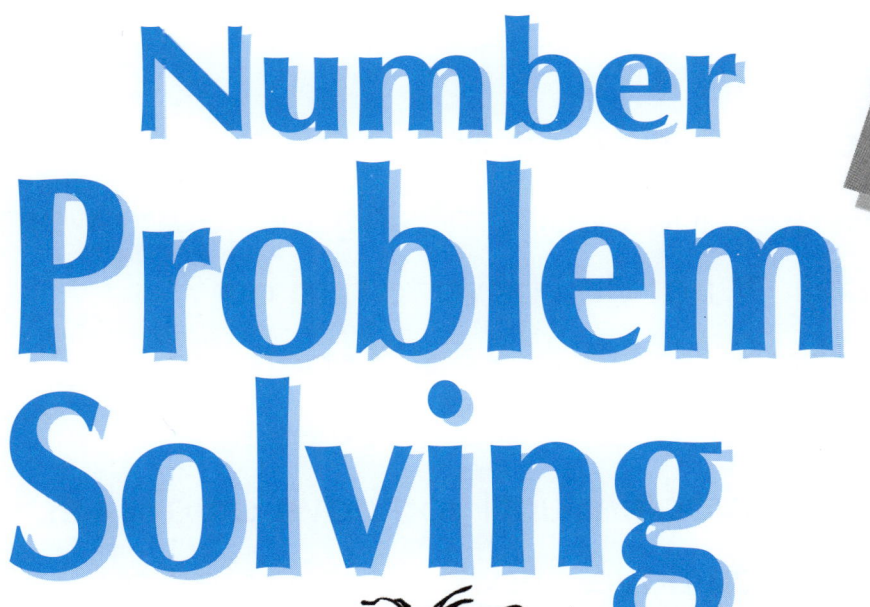

How to solve a problem

1. Read the question carefully.

2. Read the question again, making sure each word is checked.

3. Ask yourself "What do I have to find out?"

4. Draw pictures, use equipment (fingers are fine!) or write symbols or numbers.

5. Work out the problem until you have an answer.

6. Check that you have answered the question.

7. Can you check the answer by working backwards?

8. Present your answer clearly.

Remember: If you have trouble with any of these steps, go back and start again.

On the farm

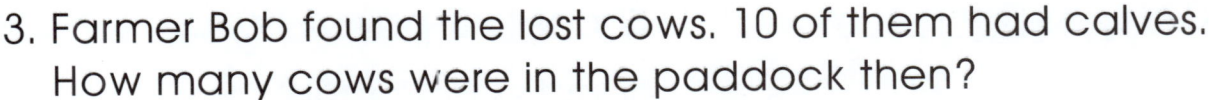

Farmer Bob had 24 cows

1. He wanted to put equal numbers into 4 paddocks.
   How many were in each paddock?
   Show your working out.

_____

2. 16 cows got out one day.
   How many were left?

_____

3. Farmer Bob found the lost cows. 10 of them had calves.
   How many cows were in the paddock then?

_____

4. What number facts can you write about 24?

_____

_____

Magic Squares

		8
	5	
	7	

Use only numbers 1 — 9.
Use each number once only.
Each row must add to 15.
Each column must add to 15.
Each diagonal must add to 15.

		7
	6	
	10	

Use only numbers 2 — 10.
Use each number once only.
Each row must add to 18.
Each column must add to 18.
Each diagonal must add to 18.

How many?

Days in 1 week? _____

10s in 50? _____

Double 18? _____

Weeks in 1 month? _____

4 groups of 5? _____

5s in 20? _____

Tens in 136? _____

Months in a year? _____

Days in 1 weekend? _____

Shoes in 7 pairs? _____

Minutes in 1 hour? _____

Half of 48? _____

Days in 1 fortnight? _____

Seconds in 1 minute? _____

Magic Triangles

Each side of the magic triangle must add to the same number.

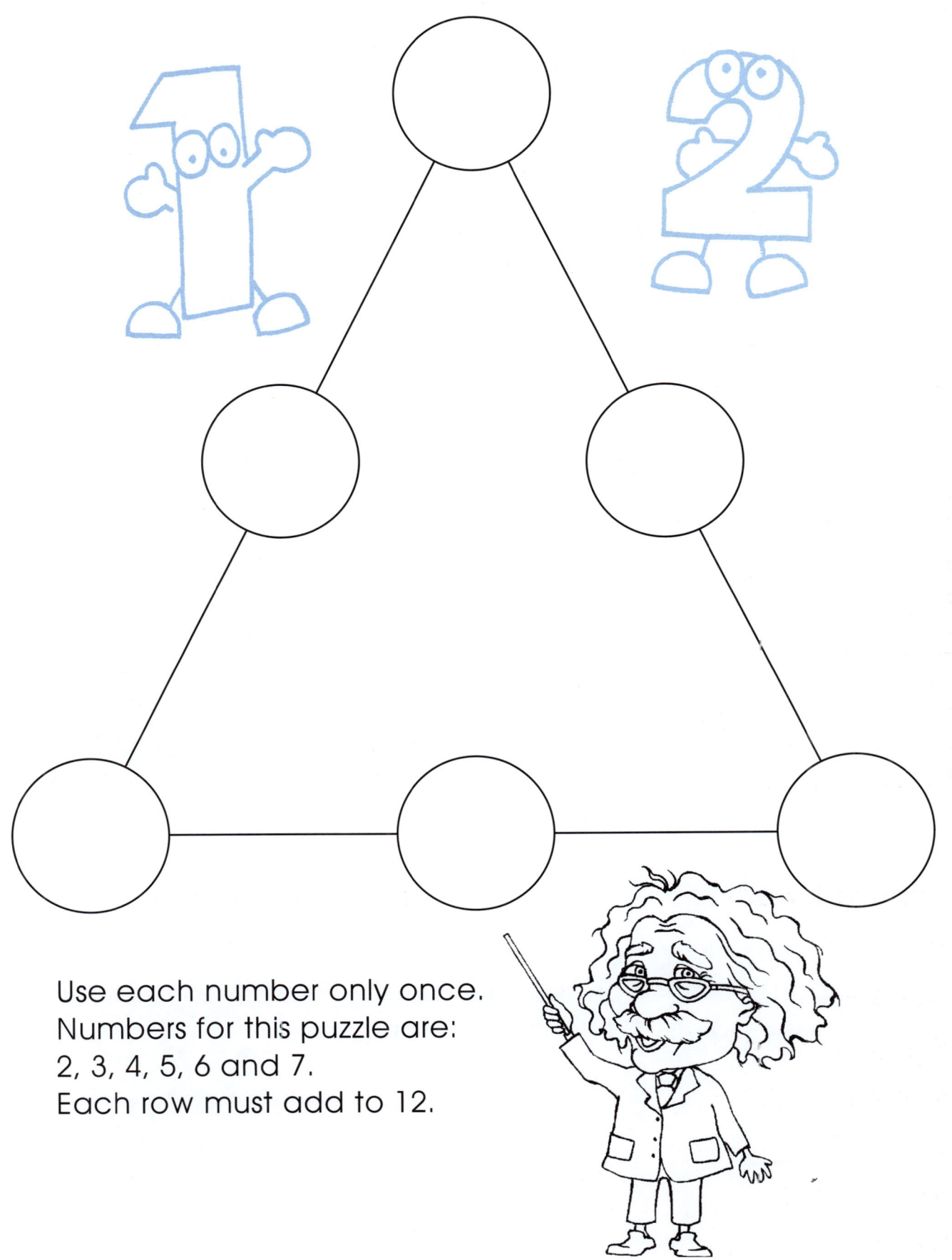

Use each number only once.
Numbers for this puzzle are:
2, 3, 4, 5, 6 and 7.
Each row must add to 12.

Problem Solving

Read carefully. Write the sums that helped you find the answers.

1. Georgia had 30 sweets. She shared them into 5 bags .
   How many lollies would be in each bag?

2. Sam had 27 basketball cards. Tom gave him 15 more.
   How many cards did Sam have?

3. Katie ran for 30 minutes. She rested and ran for 25 more minutes.
   How long was she running?

4. Natalie had 18 seeds to plant. She put 3 seeds in each hole.
   How many holes did she need?

5. The newsagent had 40 cards to sell. He sold 17 one day and 10 the next.
   How many did he have left?

6. In a basketball game. Sam scored 10, Matt scored 8 and Tom scored 10.
   How many points did the team score?

What number am I?

1. I have 3 digits.
   All the digits are odd. (not even)
   The tens digits is a 3.
   The hundreds digit is a
   multiple of 3.
   The units digit is 2 less than
   the hundreds digit.
   What number am I? _____

2. I began as 4 x 5.
   I lost 6.
   I was divided by 2.
   I multiplied by 3.
   I am _____

3. I am an even number.
   I am more than 16.
   I am less than 24.
   I am a multiple of 5.
   I am _____

4. I have 2 digits.
   My digits are the same.
   I am a multiple of 11.
   The digits add to 10.
   I am _____

5. I began as 6 x 4.
   I lost 4.
   I was divided by 4.
   I multiplied by 6.
   I am _____

6. I am an odd number.
   I lam more than 20.
   I am less than 30.
   I am a multiple of 5.
   I am _____

Number Patterns

Finish these number patterns.

3, 5, 7, _____, 11, _____, _____, 17.

28, 26, 24, _____, 20, _____, _____, 14.

9, 13, 17, _____, 25, 29, _____, _____, _____.

What is the number pattern? Write it using words.

6, 8, 10, 12, 14　　Add 2

30, 25, 20, 15, 10, 5 _____

13, 19, 25, 31, 37 _____

2, 4, 8, 16, 32 _____

Draw the groups.	Write how many.
5 groups of 3	_____
2 groups of 8	_____
4 groups of 6	_____
7 groups of 2	_____

Fun with numbers

The year 1961 can be written upside down and still look the same. The next time this will happen will be 6009.

Magic Triangle

Each side of the magic triangle must add to the same number.

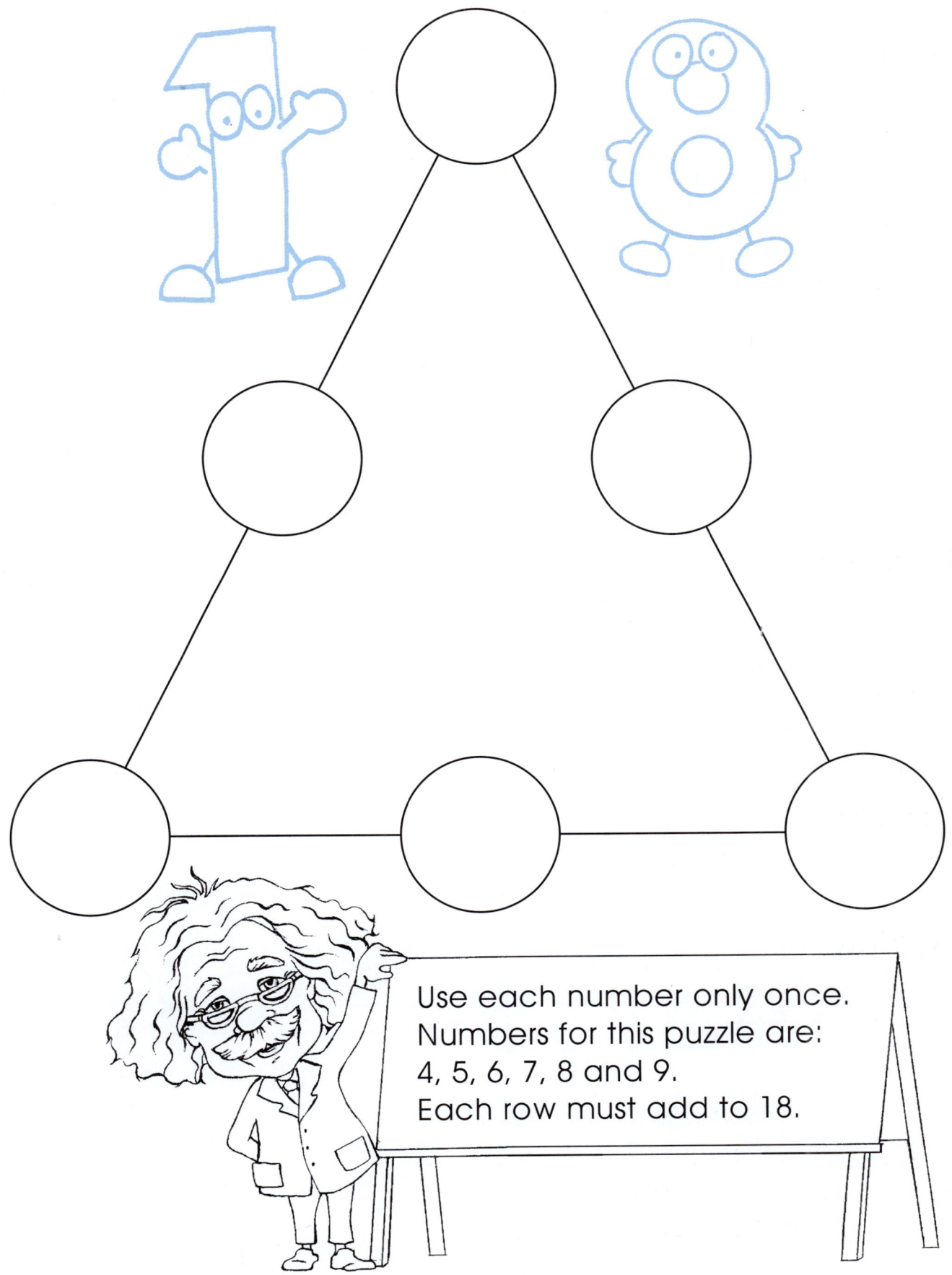

Use each number only once.
Numbers for this puzzle are:
4, 5, 6, 7, 8 and 9.
Each row must add to 18.

Problem Solving

Read carefully. Write the sums that helped you find the answers.

1. Sophie had 78 marbles. She gave 26 to Francesca .
   How many marbles were left?

2. Madeleine had 5 dogs. 2 ran away.
   How many dogs were left?

3. 21 turtles each had 1 baby.
   How many turtles were there altogether?

4. There were 20 students in 2G. 5 students were away sick.
   How many were at school?

5. In the hospital nursery, 13 boys and 15 girls were born on the
   same day. This was 5 more babies than had ever been born
   on the same day.
   What was the old record of births in one day?

6. Draw this problem. 3 oranges and 4 apples
   and 2 bananas. How many fruit altogether?

Magic Triangle

Each side of the magic triangle must add to the same number.

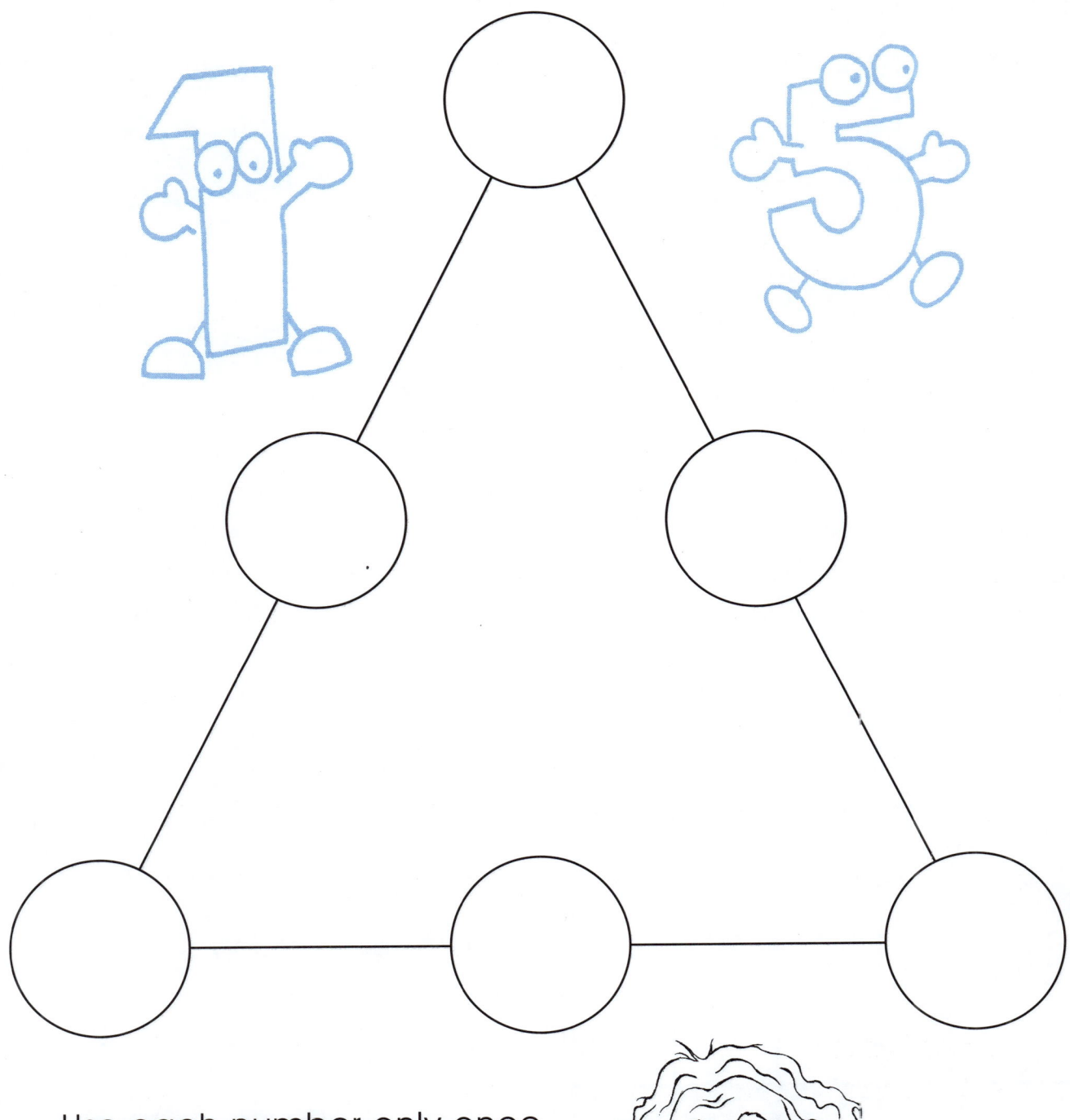

Use each number only once.
Numbers for this puzzle are:
3, 4, 5, 6, 7 and 8.
Each row must add to 15.

Look carefully

How many squares can you see in this square?

Cross number puzzle

<table>
<tr><td>■</td><td>1</td><td>2</td><td>■</td><td>3</td><td></td><td>■</td></tr>
<tr><td>4</td><td></td><td>5</td><td></td><td></td><td>■</td><td>7</td></tr>
<tr><td>8</td><td>9</td><td>■</td><td>■</td><td>■</td><td>10</td><td></td></tr>
<tr><td>■</td><td>11</td><td></td><td>■</td><td>12</td><td></td><td>■</td></tr>
<tr><td>13</td><td></td><td>■</td><td>■</td><td></td><td>■</td><td>■</td></tr>
</table>

Across
1. $11 \times 9 =$
3. half of 46 =
5. $200 + 60 + 4 =$
8. $8 \times 7 =$
10. $17 \times 3 =$
11. 7 groups of 7
12. $40 \div 4 =$
13. $28 - 14 =$

Down
2. $90 + 2 =$
3. $2 \times 12 =$
4. $50 - 25 =$
7. $7 + 7 + 7 =$
9. $600 + 40 + 4 =$
10. half of 100
12. $3 \times 5 =$

Calendar Work

MARCH						
Sun	Mon	Tue	Wed	Thu	Fri	Sat
			1	2	3	4
5	6	7	8	9	10	11
12	13	14	15	16	17	18
19	20	21	22	23	24	25
26	27	28	29	30	31	

1. How many Wednesdays in March? _____
2. What is the date, 13 days after March 8th? _____
3. What is the the last Saturday in March? _____
4. April 1st falls on what day? _____
5. List the Saturday dates _____
6. Which day is St. Patrick's day? _____
7. What is the date 2 weeks before 1st March? _____
8. How many of the Tuesdays have even numbers? _____
9. What is the date 5 days before 11th March? _____

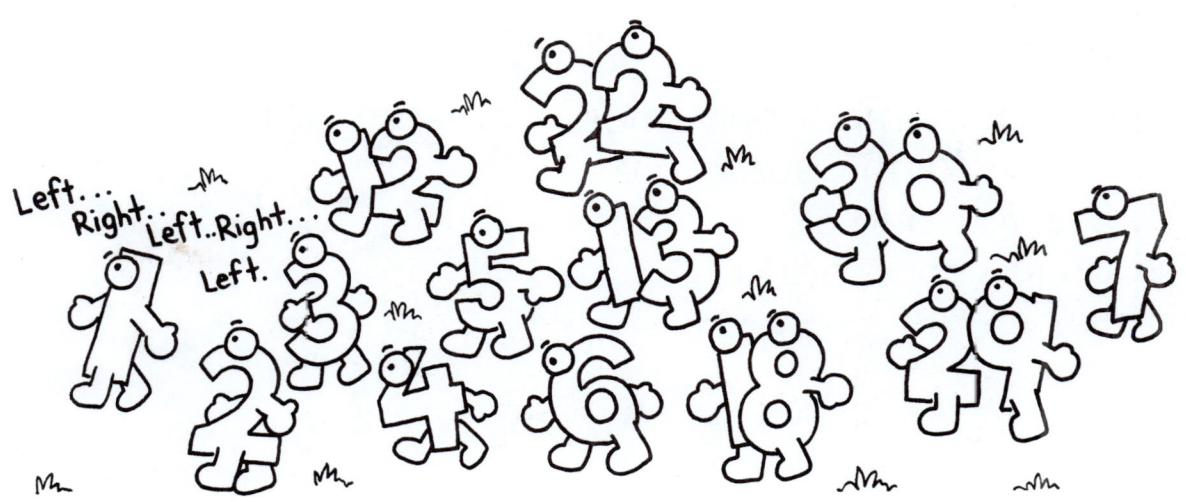

Left... Right.. Left..Right... Left.

109

Magic Triangle

Each side of the magic triangle must add to the same number.

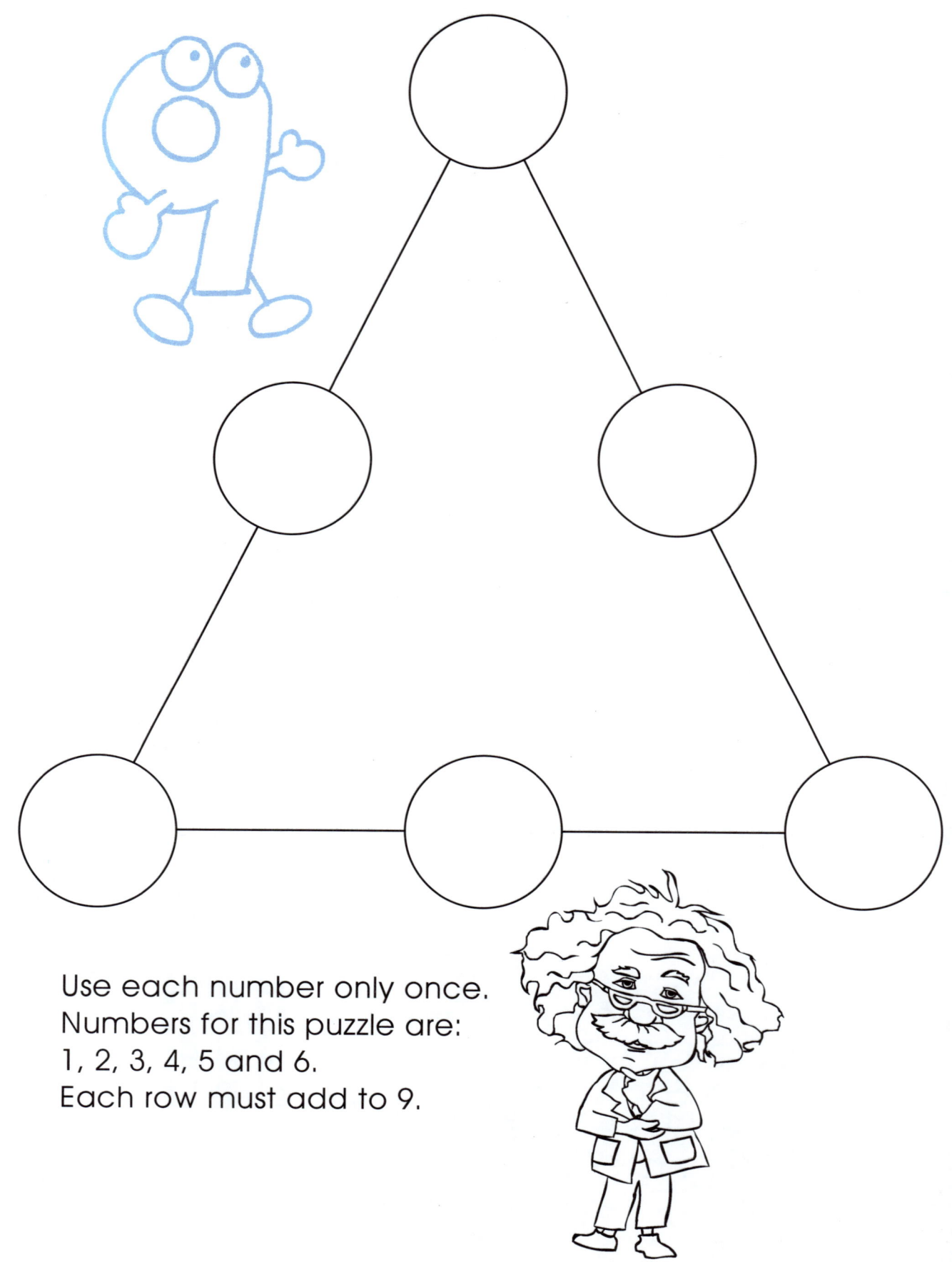

Use each number only once.
Numbers for this puzzle are:
1, 2, 3, 4, 5 and 6.
Each row must add to 9.

Shopping

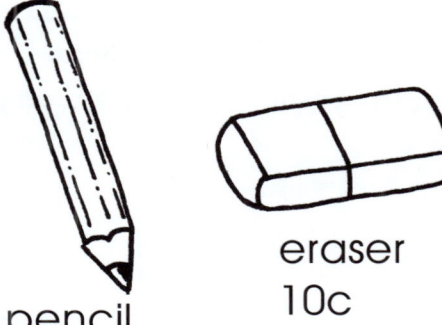

pencil
5c

eraser
10c

note book
20c

ruler
15c

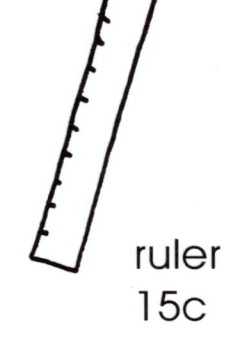

scissors
25c

How much would it cost to buy
1. 1 pencil + 1 eraser? _____
2. 1 note book + 1 pencil? _____
3. 1 pair scissors + 1 note book? _____
4. 1 pencil + 1 eraser + 1 ruler? _____
5. 1 pair scissors + 1 pencil? _____

Where does Mary live?

Can you work out where I live from the clues?

The number of my house has 2 digits in it.
The digits are not the same.
It is an odd number.
The number is in the three times tables.
The number is between 20 and 40.
The digits add up to 9.
What is the number on my house?

Mary's house number

What number am I?

1. I am greater than 12.
   I am less than 20.
   I am an even number.
   I can be divided by 4.
   I am _____

2. I am greater than 17.
   I am less than 22.
   I am an odd number.
   I can be divided by 3.
   I am _____

3. I am half way between
   6 and 14.
   What number am I _____

4. I am half way between
   2 and 16.
   What number am I _____

5. I am half way between
   10 and 24.
   What number am I _____

6. I am greater than 50.
   I am less than 60.
   I am an even number.
   I am double 27.
   I am _____

7. I am greater than 40.
   I am less than 45.
   I am an even number.
   I can be divided by 6.
   I am _____

8. I am half way between
   12 and 26.
   What number am I? _____

Working with areas

Guess how many of these small squares will fit into these shapes?

1. My guess ____ squares

2. My guess ____ squares

3. My guess ____ squares

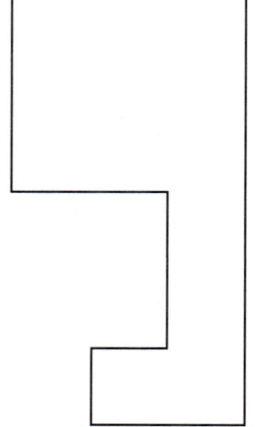

4. My guess
   ____ squares

Find 3 numbers which add up to 16

1.

4	15	10	8	2	6

_____ + _____ + _____ = 16

2. Write the numbers in order from the smallest to the largest.

_____ _____ _____ _____ _____ _____

Find 4 numbers which add up to 21

3.

11	2	9	7	1	5	16

_____ + _____ + _____ + _____ = 21

4. Write the numbers in order from the smallest to the largest.

_____ _____ _____ _____ _____ _____

Complete these sums

1. 20 – 9 = ☐☐

2. 45 – 20 = ☐☐

3. 28 + 17 = ☐☐

4. 400 + 40 + 1 = ☐☐☐

5. 36 + 7 = ☐☐

6. 30 – 15 = ☐☐

7. 69 – 64 = ☐

8. 10 – 6 = ☐

9. 6 x 9 = ☐☐

10. 15 – 4 = ☐☐

11. 12 x 10 = ☐☐☐

12. 4 groups of 11 = ☐☐

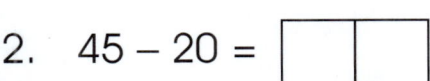
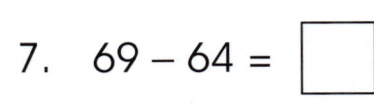

Tens and Units

35 = ☐ tens ☐ units   66 = ☐ tens ☐ units

27 = ☐ tens ☐ units   49 = ☐ tens ☐ units

Match these words and numbers

54	sixty-three	29	forty-five
78	ninety-six	82	thirty-seven
63	seventy-eight	37	twenty-nine
96	fifty-four	45	eighty-two

Look carefully at these numbers.
And answer the questions.

How many units in 42? _____
How many tens in 68? _____
How many hundreds in 215? _____

tens

Write the numbers in expanded form.

256 = _____ + _____ + _____

471 = _____ + _____ + _____

837 = _____ + _____ + _____

503 = _____ + _____ + _____

units

Look carefully at these numbers.
And answer the questions.

How many tens in 156? _____
How many hundreds in 604? _____
How many units in 76? _____

APRIL

Sun	Mon	Tue	Wed	Thu	Fri	Sat
						1
2	3	4	5	6	7	8
9	10	11	12	13	14	15
16	17	18	19	20	21	22
23	24	25	26	27	28	29
30						

MAY

Sun	Mon	Tue	Wed	Thu	Fri	Sat
	1	2	3	4	5	6
7	8	9	10	11	12	13
14	15	16	17	18	19	20
21	22	23	24	25	26	27
28	29	30	31			

1. How many days in April? _____
2. How many days in May? _____
3. What is the date 1 week after 20th April? _____
4. What is the date 6 days before 16th May? _____
5. What are the dates for all the Saturdays in April? _____
6. How many Wednesdays are there in May? _____
7. What day is it on June 1st? _____
8. How many days between 7th April and 21st April? _____
9. May is the _____ month of the year?
10. Which days in April occurs 5 times? _____

At the Canteen

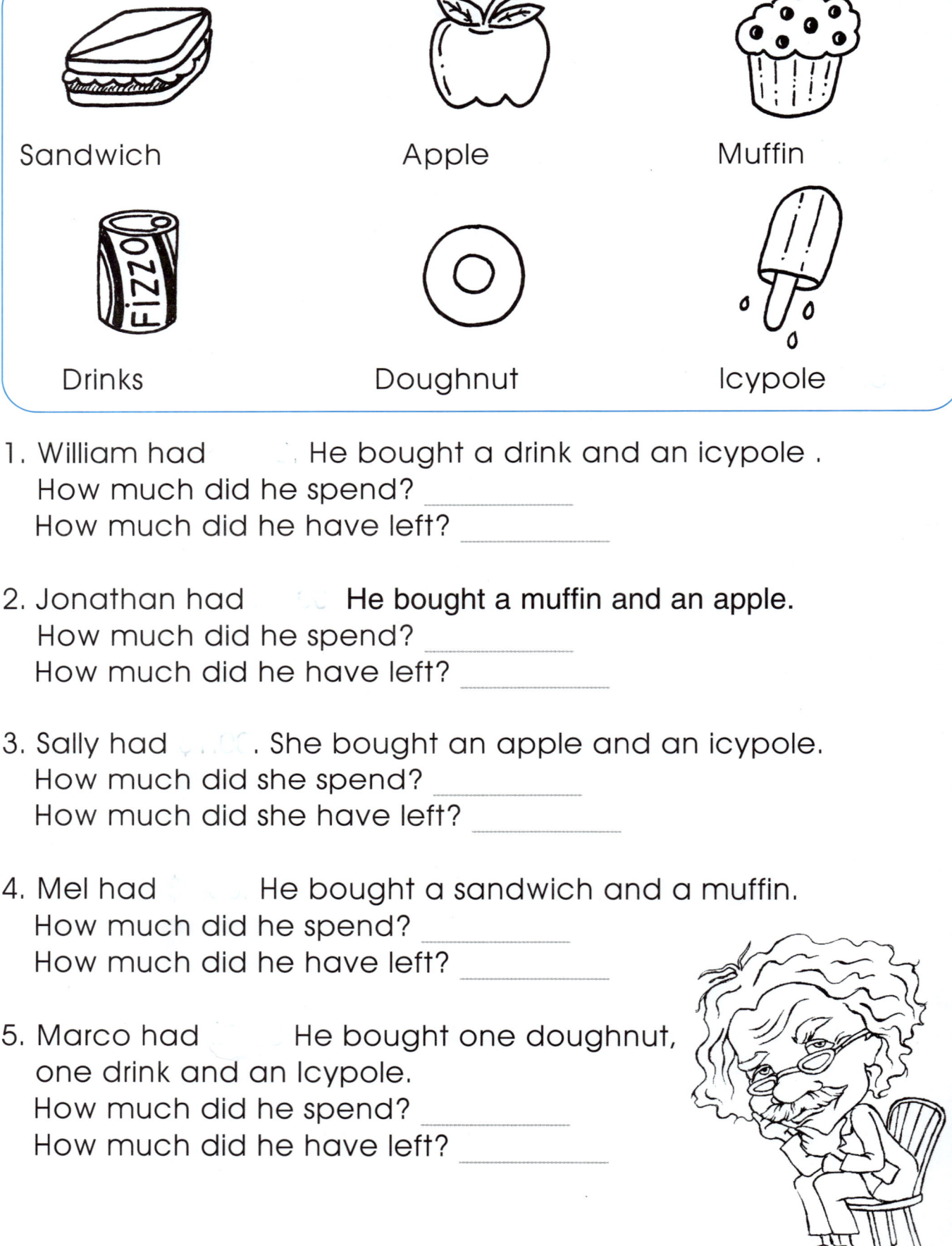

Sandwich

Apple

Muffin

Drinks

Doughnut

Icypole

1. William had   . He bought a drink and an icypole .
   How much did he spend? _____
   How much did he have left? _____

2. Jonathan had   He bought a muffin and an apple.
   How much did he spend? _____
   How much did he have left? _____

3. Sally had   . She bought an apple and an icypole.
   How much did she spend? _____
   How much did she have left? _____

4. Mel had   He bought a sandwich and a muffin.
   How much did he spend? _____
   How much did he have left? _____

5. Marco had   He bought one doughnut,
   one drink and an Icypole.
   How much did he spend? _____
   How much did he have left? _____

Sort the numbers in the buckets into the right place

Between 3 and 7	Between 7 and 10	Bucket: 4 8 9 5
		Odd
		Even

Counting by 5s	Counting by 3s	Bucket: 9 10 12 15
		Odd
		Even

Bucket: 3 2 8 7	Less than 5	More than 5
Odd		
Even		

Bucket: 10 17 13 18	More than 15	Less than 15
Odd		
Even		

Make up your own

		Bucket

		Bucket

Read the clues carefully. Which number am I?

1. I am not greater than 400.
   I do not have 5 tens.
   I am less than 200.
   I am more than 100.
   I am _____

125	68	224
	516	
157		
		348
427	259	

2. I am greater than 200.
   I am less than 400.
   I am an even number.
   I do not have 6 in the tens place.
   The sum of my digits is 9.
   I am _____

536	147	234
261	95	408
176	361	319

3. I am not greater than 500.
   I am not 4 hundreds + 2 tens and
   6 units.
   I have 3 tens.
   I am less than 300.
   I am _____

624	238	591
426	332	
219	435	378

Complete these sums

1. $10 + 8 =$ ☐☐

2. $14 + 14 =$ ☐☐

3. $80 \times 10 =$ ☐☐☐

4. $100 + 20 + 5 =$ ☐☐☐

5. Double $18 =$ ☐☐

6. $300 + 300 =$ ☐☐☐

7. Half of $80 =$ ☐☐

8. $3 \times 4 =$ ☐☐

9. $2 \times 1 =$ ☐

10. Double $42 =$ ☐☐

11. Ten plus two $=$ ☐☐

12. 5 groups of $6 =$ ☐☐

Sharing into equal groups.

1.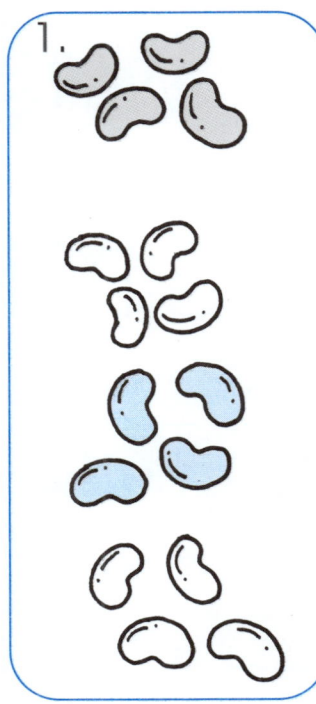

2.

3.

4.

16 ÷ 4 = _____   _____   _____   _____

Show your working out.

5. Victoria picked 36 flowers. She put them into 3 vases.
   How many were in each vase?

_____

6. Michael had 16 golf clubs. He had 2 bags to carry them.
   How many did he put in each bag?

_____

7. Greg hit 24 tennis balls. He packed them into 4 containers.
   How many balls were in each container?

_____

8. Lucy had 12 hair ribbons.
   How many pairs did she have?

_____

Work this out

Write the numbers 1 - 10 in the circles.
Use each number only once.
Each line including the centre numbers
must add to 21.

Work this out

Write the numbers 1 - 10 in the circles.
Use each number only once.
Each line including the centre numbers
must add to 23.

Work this out

Write the numbers
1 - 9 in the circles.
Use each number only once.
Each line including the centre numbers must add to 25.

What's the scariest number?
Seven.
Why?
Because seven ate nine!

Yum!

Problem solving

Read carefully. Write the sums that helped you find the answers.

1. Janet walked to the shop and back home. The shop is 250 steps from her house.
   How many steps did she walk?

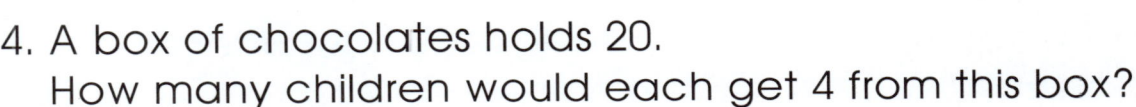

2. There are one dozen (12) eggs in each box.
   How many eggs would you get in 4 boxes?

3. Spring rolls come in packs of 6.
   How many spring rolls would there be in 6 packs?

4. A box of chocolates holds 20.
   How many children would each get 4 from this box?

5. Fruit box drinks are in packs of 4.
   How many packs would I need to give 40 children a drink?

6. The baker baked 100 loaves of bread he sold 89 loaves.
   How many were left?

7. Vincent has 45 friends to whom he should give Christmas cards.
   How many packs of 15 cards must he buy?

Time for fun

Telling the time is something we need to learn
Then we will know when it's meal time for our favourite TV show
and time to play with friends.

| When the long hand is on the 12 it's o'clock. | When the long hand is on the 6 it's half past. | When the long hand is on the 3 it's quarter past. | When the long hand is on the 9 it's quarter to. |

Now look at each clock and write the time.

1 hour before   Tic Toc   1/2 hour after

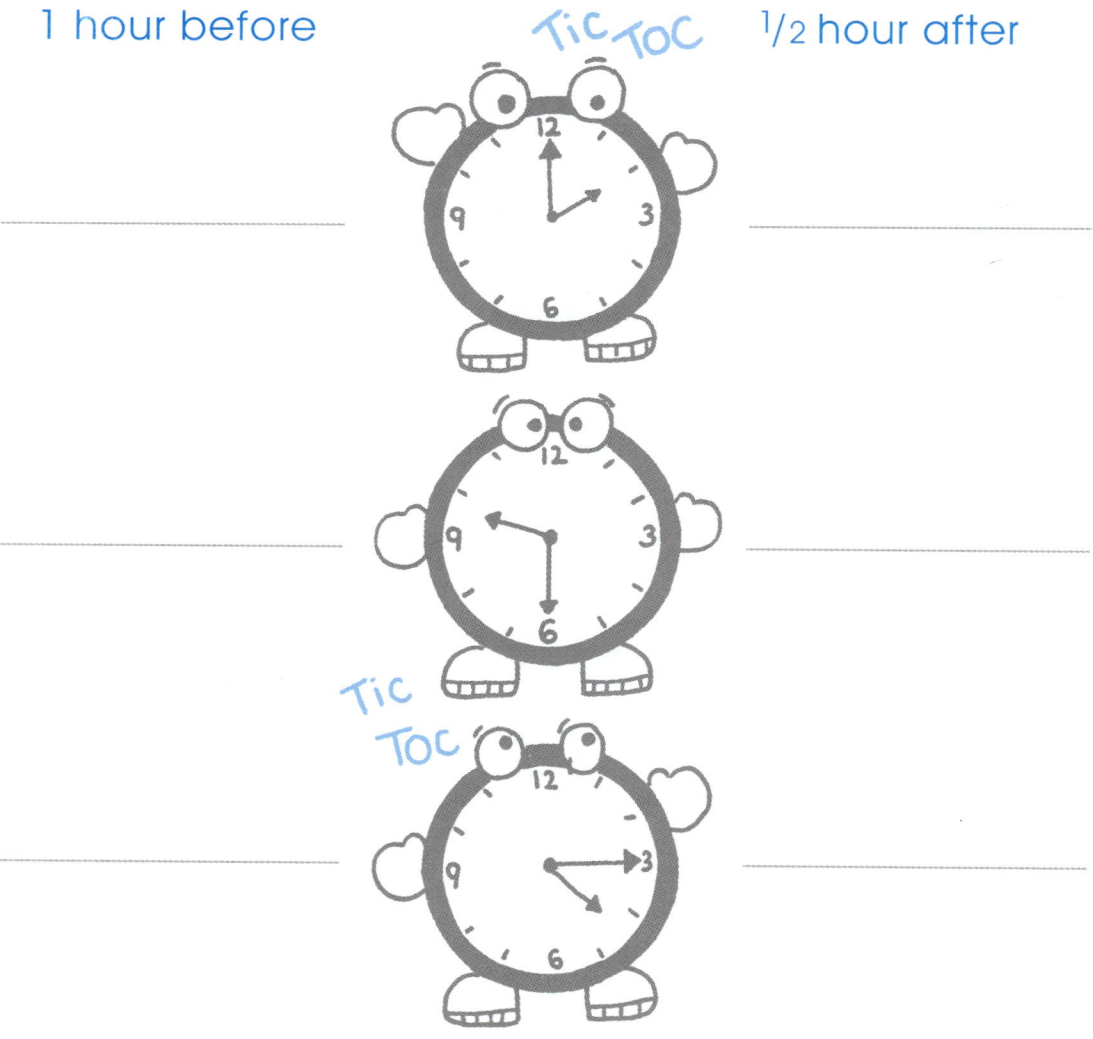

_____   _____

_____   _____

Tic
TOC

_____   _____

Time for fun

Draw the hour and the minute hands on these clocks.

Half past 1   6 O'clock   quarter to 7   quarter past 4

Think carefully about these problems.

1. Jack left home at 1.30pm. His trip took him 2 ½ hours.
   What time did he arrive? _____

2. Lisa had to eat her lunch 1 ¼ hours before she went swimming
   at 2.00pm.
   What time did she eat? _____

3. Write the times in order from earliest to latest.
   6.30pm   11.45am   6.30am   10.45pm   7.00pm   8.30am

_____

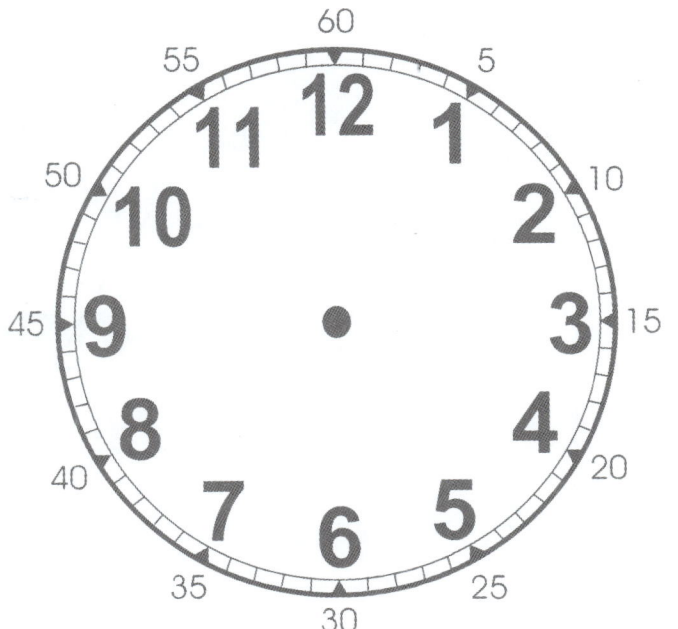

How many minutes?

from 5 to 10 _____

from 5 to 15 _____

from 5 to 20 _____

from 5 to 25 _____

from 5 to 45 _____

from 5 to 60 _____

from 25 to 40 _____

125

Card games?

There is a card game called 21. In it you must add the cards till you get 21. Here are some to practice.

9 + 2 + ☐ = 21

6 + 8 + ☐ = 21

4 + 9 + ☐ = 21

7 + 5 + ☐ = 21

3 + 8 + ☐ = 21

10 + 4 + ☐ = 21

ANSWER PAGE

Page 99.
1) $24 \div 4 = 6$
2) $24 - 16 = 8$
3) $24 + 10 = 34$
4) $24 \times 2 = 24$
   $24 \div 2 = 24$
   $12 + 12 = 24$
   $24 - 12 = 12$
   $8 \times 3 = 24$
   $24 \div 3 = 8$
   $6 \times 4 = 24$
   $24 \div 4 = 6$

Page 100.

4	3	8
9	5	1
2	7	6

9	2	7
4	6	8
5	10	3

How many?
7, 5, 36, 4, 20, 4, 13, 12, 2, 14, 60, 24, 14, 60

Page 101.

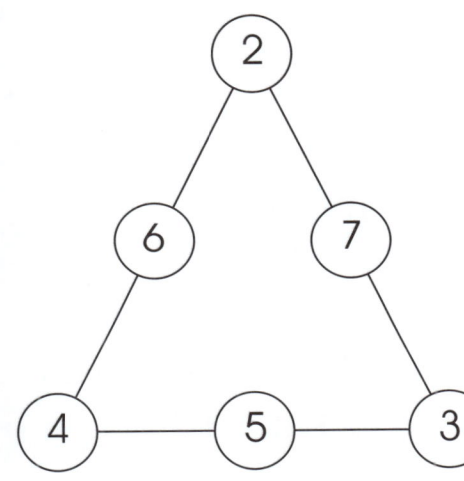

Page 102.
1) $30 \div 5 = 6$
2) $27 + 15 = 42$
3) $30 + 25 = 55$
4) $18 \div 3 = 6$
5) $40 - 17 = 23$
   $23 - 10 = 13$
   13 left
6) $10 + 8 + 10 = 28$

Page 103.
1) 937
2) 21
3) 20
4) 55
5) 30
6) 25

Page 104. Number Patterns
Finish these
number patterns
9, 13, 15
22, 18, 16
21, 33, 37, 41
What is the number
pattern?
Take 5
Add 6
Times 2
Write how many
15, 16, 24, 14

Page 105.

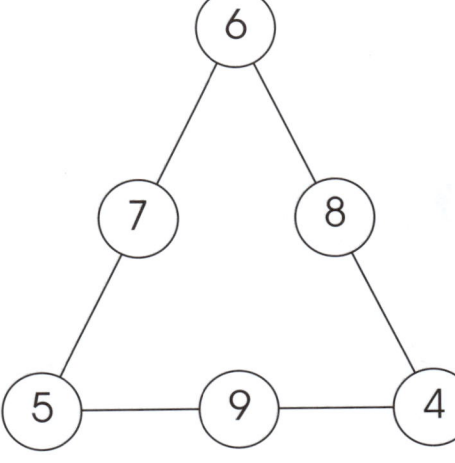

Page 106.
1) $78 - 26 = 52$
2) $5 - 2 = 3$
3) $21 + 21 = 42$
4) $20 - 5 = 15$
5) $13 + 15 = 28$
   $28 - 5 = 23$
   23 was old
   record
6) $3 + 4 + 2 = 9$

ANSWER PAGE

Page 107.

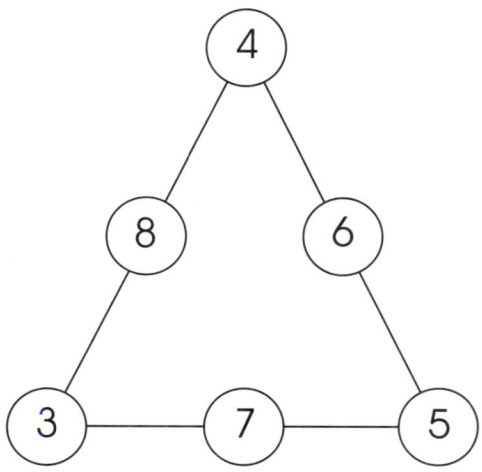

Page 108.
30 squares

Cross number puzzle

Across	Down
1) 99	2) 92
3) 23	3) 24
5) 264	4) 25
8) 56	7) 21
10) 51	9) 644
11) 49	10) 50
12) 10	12) 15
13) 14	

Page 109.
1) 5
2) 21st March
3) 25th March
4) Saturday
5) 4, 11, 18, 25
6) Friday
7) 14th February
   or 15th February
   in leap year
8) 2
9) 6th March

Page 110.

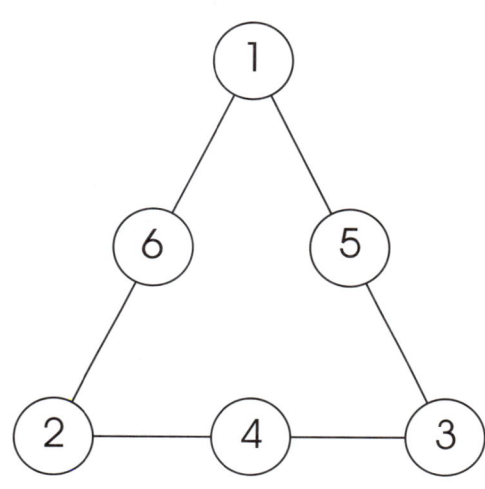

Page 111.
1) 15c
2) 25c
3) 45c
4) 30c
5) 30c

Where does Mary live?
No. 27

Page 112.
1) 16	6) 54
2) 21	7) 42
3) 10	8) 19
4) 9	
5) 17	

Working with areas
1) 6 squares
2) 7 squares
3) 8 squares
4) 13 squares

Page 113.
1) 4 + 10 + 2 = 16
   or 8 + 6 + 2 = 16
2) 2, 4, 6, 8, 10, 15
3) 11 + 2 + 7 + 1 = 21
4) 1, 2, 5, 7, 9, 11, 16

Complete these sums
1) 11	7) 5
2) 25	8) 4
3) 45	9) 54
4) 441	10) 11
5) 43	11) 120
6) 15	12) 44

ANSWER PAGE

Page 114.
Ten and Units

35 = 3 tens 5 units
27 = 2 tens 7 units
66 = 6 tens 6 units
49 = 4 tens 9 units

Match words and numbers

54—fifty-four
78—seventy-eight
63—sixty-three
29—twenty-nine
82—eighty-two
37—thirty-seven
45—forty-five

Answer the questions

2, 6, 2

Write the numbers in expanded form

256 = 200 + 50 + 6
471 = 400 + 70 + 1
837 = 800 + 30 + 7
503 = 500 + 00 + 3

Answer the questions

5, 6, 6

Page 115.
1) 30
2) 31
3) 27th April
4) 10th May
5) 1, 8, 15, 22, 29
6) 5
7) Thursday
8) 14
9) 5th
10) Saturday and Sunday

Page 116.
1) $1.25, 25c
2) $1.60, 40c
3) 80c, 20c
4) $2.30, 20c
5) $2.05, $2.95

Page 117.
Sort the numbers in the buckets into the right place

Between 3 and 7	Between 7 and 10	
5	9	Odd
4	8	Even

Bucket: 4, 8, 9, 5

	Less than 5	More than 5
Odd	3	7
Even	2	8

Bucket: 3, 2, 8, 7

Counting by 5s	Counting by 3s	
15	9	Odd
10	12	Even

Bucket: 9, 10, 12, 15

	More than 15	Less than 15
Odd	17	13
Even	18	10

Bucket: 10, 17, 13, 18

129

ANSWER PAGE

Page 118.
1) 125
2) 234
3) 238

Complete these sums
1) 18   7) 40
2) 28   8) 12
3) 800   9) 2
4) 125   10) 84
5) 36   11) 12
6) 600   12) 30

Page 119.
Sharing into the equal groups
1) 16 ÷ 4 = 4
2) 10 ÷ 2 = 5
3) 20 ÷ 5 = 4
4) 15 ÷ 3 = 5
5) 36 ÷ 3 = 12
6) 16 ÷ 2 = 8
7) 24 ÷ 4 = 6
8) 12 ÷ 2 = 6

Page 120.
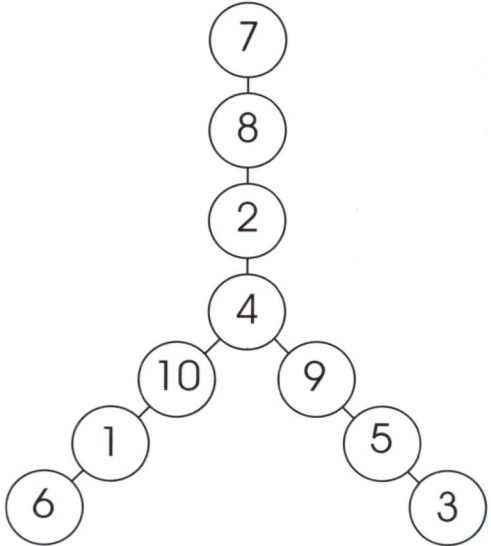

Page 121.
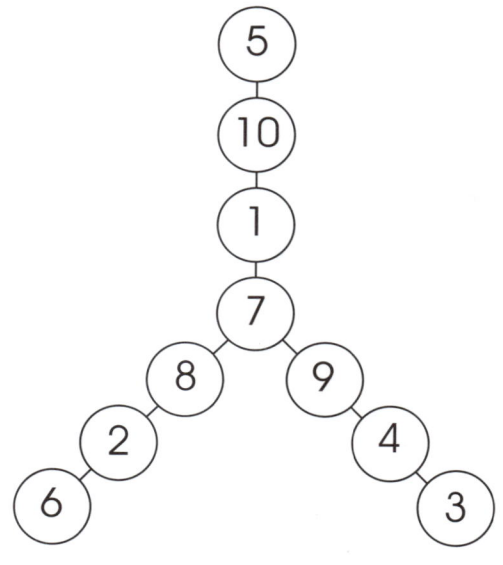

Page 122.
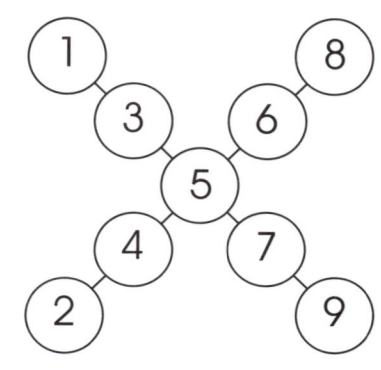

Page 123.
1) 250 + 250 = 500 steps
2) 12 x 4 = 48 eggs
3) 6 x 6 = 36 spring rolls
4) 20 ÷ 4 = 5 children
5) 40 ÷ 4 = 10 packs of fruit boxes
6) 100 – 89 = 11 loaves
7) 45 ÷ 15 = 3 packs

Page 124.
1 o'clock, half past 2
half past 8, 10 o'clock
quarter past 3, quarter to 5

Page 125.

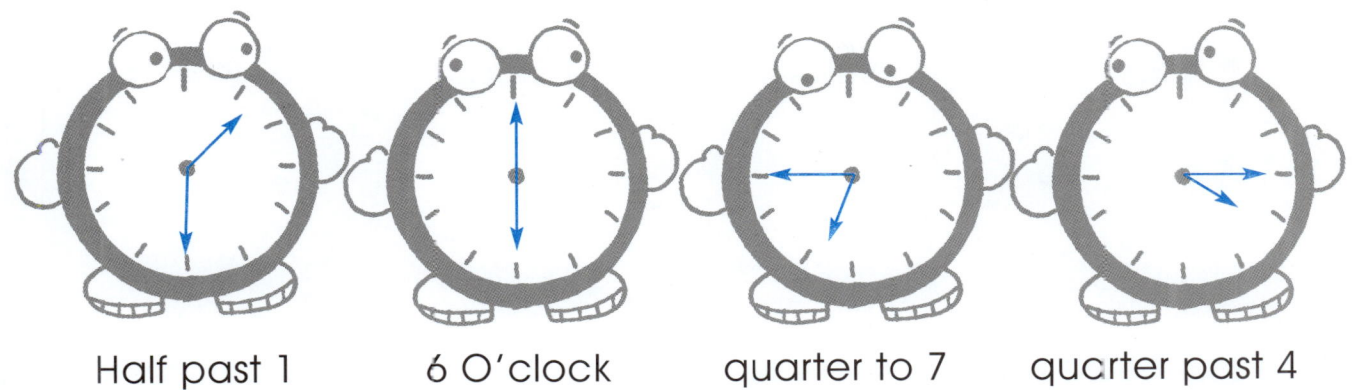

Half past 1   6 O'clock   quarter to 7   quarter past 4

1) 4.00pm
2) Quarter to 1 or 12.45pm
3) 6.30am, 8.30am, 11.45am, 6.30pm, 7.00pm, 10.45pm
How many minutes?
5, 10, 15, 20, 40, 55, 15

Page 126.
Card games
10
  7
  8
  9
10
  7

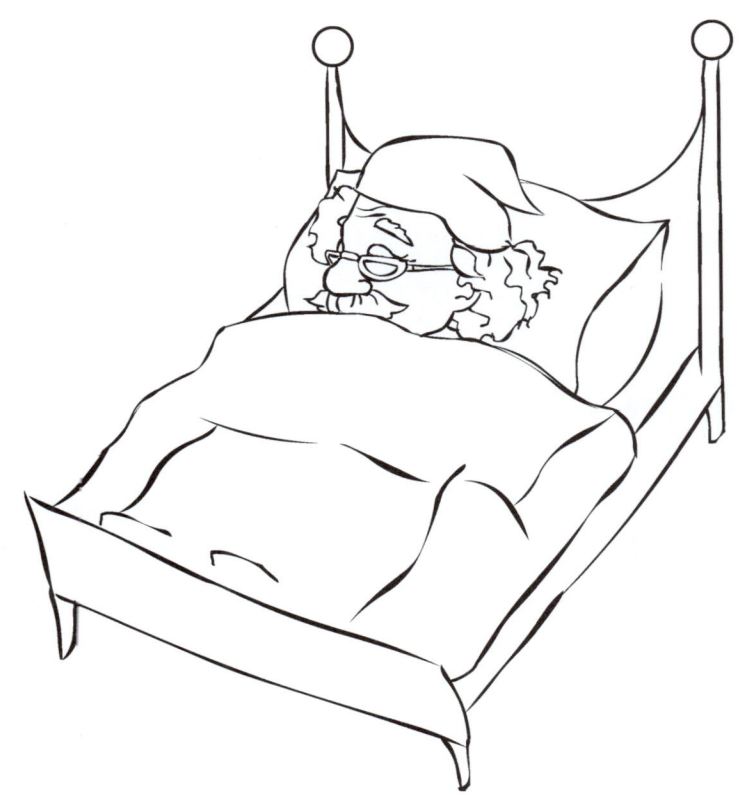